The New Conquistadors

In affection to
George Green O.B.E., Librarian
of the Hispanic and Luso Brazilian
Council, who has helped and
corrected not only me, but so many
other students of Latin American
history.

The New Conquistadors

JAN READ

Evans Brothers Limited, London

Published by Evans Brothers Limited
Montague House, Russell Square,
London WC1B 5BX

© Jan Read 1980
First published 1980

British Library Cataloguing in Publication Data
Read, Jan
      The new conquistadors.
      1. South America – History – Wars of
      Independence, 1806–1830 – Foreign participation
      2. British in South America
      I. Title
      980 .02   F2235
ISBN 0–237–45516–1

Printed and bound in Great Britain by
Fakenham Press Limited, Fakenham, Norfolk

PRA 6834

Contents

List of Illustrations

Sir Gregor McGregor (from Thomas Strangeways, *Sketch of the Mosquito Shore*, 1822)

Lancers of the Plains of Apuré (engraving from Col. J. P. Hamilton, *Travels through the Interior Provinces of Columbia*, 1828)

Simón Bolívar (engraving from Gen. Ducoudray Holstein, *Memoirs of Simon Bolivar*, 1830)

Natural bridge in the High Andes (from Alexander von Humboldt, *Personal Narrative of Travels*, 1814–29)

The High Andes (from Edmond Temple, op. cit.)

Between pages 112 and 113

Rio de Janeiro (contemporary engraving)

The Slave Market at Rio de Janeiro (engraving from Maria Graham, *Journal of a Voyage to Brazil*, 1824)

Dom Pedro I of Brazil (Museo dos Coches, Lisbon)

Lady Cochrane (miniature, by courtesy of Douglas Cochrane Esq.)

The Palace of San Cristovão, near Rio de Janeiro, (engraving from Maria Graham, op. cit.)

Admiral Brown in old age (lithograph by N. Desmadryl)

Naval encounter between Admirals Brown and Norton (contemporary engraving)

J. G. de Francia (engraving from J. P. and W. P. Robertson, *Letters on Paraguay*, 1838–9)

Unless stated otherwise, the illustrations are reproduced by kind permission of the Hispanic Council Library and The University of St. Andrews.

Author's Note

IT would be pretentious to write a long preface to a book which is itself but a preface to the intricate history of the campaigns which freed South America from the centuries' long domination of Spain and Portugal.

I have tried to explain the events leading up to the revolt of the colonists, to sketch the course of the conflict in the different parts of South America and to outline official British policy towards the emergent republics; but the burden of the book is to describe the unofficial intervention of the thousands of English, Scots and Irish who participated either from idealistic or mercenary motives. If there is a tendency to magnify their achievements, it is unintentional and because this *is* primarily an account of the British adventurers and not the war in general.

Since the liberation movement in Mexico followed a very different course and British volunteers were not involved, the book deals only with South America. For similar reasons, it does not embrace the Spanish Antilles (the Dominican Republic and Cuba), which broke away later. Brazil, on the other hand, is included because Admiral Cochrane and his squadron, largely British-manned, made an important contribution towards breaking the last ties with Portugal.

I am grateful to Mr Gerald S. Graham and Professor R. A. Humphreys for the use of the short extract from *The Navy and South America*, Navy Records Society, 1962; to Professor Humphreys for the quotation from *Liberation in South America*, Athlone Press, 1952; and to Senhor Prado Maia for the quotation from *A Marinha de Guerra do Brasil na Colonia e no Imperio*, Rio de Janeiro, 1965.

9

Prologue
The GOLDEN LEGEND

IT was a Spanish soldier, a certain Martínez, set adrift by his companions while exploring the Orinoco, who first brought back tales of a fabulous city of gold somewhere in the interior of South America. In describing the repeated fruitless efforts to locate El Dorado, Michael Mulhall, author of an early account of *The English in South America*, supplies the picturesque information that 'this name was first applied, not to the country, but to the King, Cuarica, who dwelt in palaces with pillars of solid gold, whose attire was in keeping with the glitter of his dominions; he wore instead of clothes a coating of balsamic gum, with a sprinkling of gold dust blown upon his person through a hollow tube twice a day, which gave His Majesty the look of a Golden King. Every night he washed off the gilding, and was regilt next morning. It was plain that gold must abound in such a country; some placed it between Guayana and the river Parima, others at the foot of the Andes.'

Although the best efforts of the Spaniards failed to discover the golden city of Manoa, the presence of prodigious mineral wealth in the form of gold and silver proved to be true enough. Unfortunately the myth of El Dorado was to bedevil the history of South America for centuries. According to one observer, Captain Basil Hall of the Royal Navy, writing in 1824, 'The sole purpose for which the Americas existed was held to be that of collecting together the precious metals for the Spaniards; and if the wild horses and cattle, which overran the country, could have been trained to perform the same office, the inhabitants might have been altogether dispensed with, and the colonial system would have been perfect.' The misfortunes of the Indians stemmed from two practices imposed by the conquering Spaniards: the *mita* and the *repartimiento*.

The *mita* was enforced labour, exacted in the first place for a period of one year. Hundreds of thousands of Indians were regularly employed in the mines, of which, at one time, there were no less than fourteen hundred in Peru alone. The *mitayo's* pittance of four *reales* a day did not even cover his miserable diet and lodging, so that he ended his year in debt to his employer, who would then refuse to release him. In the words of another contemporary, John Miller, 'each succeeding year found him more and more deeply

10

involved . . . Languishing under the baneful effects of the transition from the genial air and exercise of his native abode, to the noxious exhalations and exhausting labour of the mines, worn out with fatigue, grief and disease, the wretched mitayo in a few months generally yielded to his fate, and found a refuge in the grave.' In writing *The Memoirs of General Miller*, his famous brother, he estimates that 'eight million two hundred and eighty-five thousand Indians thus perished in the mines of Peru'.

The *repartimiento* was instituted with the best intention of making available necessities to the Indians at fair prices. However, it was not long before corrupt *corregidores*, exercising a near monopoly, were unloading damaged foodstuffs and goods otherwise unsaleable. 'One instance will illustrate the system. Some foolish speculator in Europe had sent out, amongst other things, a consignment of spectacles, which lay useless in the stores of a merchant in Lima. After every hope of disposing of them had failed, in a country in which people retain their eyesight unimpaired to a very late period in life, a corregidor was applied to, who, upon issuing an order that no Indian in his district should attend divine service, upon certain festivals, unless ornamented with spectacles, found means to dispose of the whole of them at an enormous profit.'

It would be oversimplifying to suggest that all of the Spanish and Portuguese arrived in the New World simply to amass gold and material possessions. In 1537 Pope Paul III had decreed that the native Indians were 'truly men' and should be converted to Christianity by preaching and by 'good and holy living'. The Conquistadors commonly read out to the uncomprehending heathens a *requerimiento* – in effect, a summary of the tenets of Spanish Catholicism – and failing their instant submission, proceeded to the attack; but there were administrators and churchmen, such as the saintly Bartolomé de las Casas, who, to their own disadvantage, genuinely concerned themselves with the plight of the Indians. In parts of what are now Uruguay, Paraguay and the Argentine the Jesuits established model colonies. Their missions were a standing reproach to the often venal clergy and in 1766–7 were closed by order of the Council of the Indies in Madrid.

Although at this point discontent was rife among the colonists, the oppressed and demoralized Indians were no longer a threat to the *status quo*. Both in Spanish America and in Brazil, it was the creoles, native-born Americans of pure Spanish or Portuguese descent, who most bitterly resented a state of affairs where *peninsulares* were sent from Europe to occupy the key administrative positions.

THE NEW CONQUISTADORS

On the tomb of Columbus in Seville there is an inscription referring to 'ungrateful America'. Spain and Portugal were slow to understand the reasons which impelled their American possessions to break away or to forgive them for their defection. But countries, like children, grow up and finally jib at outside control; and the struggles for independence, in which freebooting British soldiers and sailors played so important a role, had been brewing before the turn of the nineteenth century. The grievances of both the Spanish and Portuguese colonists sprang from the attempts of the mother countries to impose strict control long after they were in a position to do so – although, in Brazil, complaints were allayed by the transfer of the seat of government to Rio de Janeiro after the French invasion of Portugal and the arrival of the royal family in 1807.

The vast Spanish domains were divided into viceroyalties, captain-generalships, *intendencias* and smaller units of administration (see map, page 13). When the inhabitants of Buenos Aires declared independence in 1816, their Manifesto stated that:

> All public offices and employments belonged exclusively to the Spaniards; and although Americans were equally called to them by the laws, they were appointed only in rare instances, and even then, not until they had satiated the cupidity of the court by enormous sums of money. Of one-hundred-and-seventy Viceroys that have governed the country, only four have been Americans; and of the six-hundred-and-ten captains-general and governors, all but fourteen have been Spaniards. The same took place in every other post of importance; and even amongst the common clerks of office, it was rare to meet with Americans.

Above all, the colonists resented restrictions on agriculture and commerce. Thus Captain Basil Hall reports that 'even so late as 1803 . . . orders were received from Spain to root up all the vines in the northern provinces, because the Cadiz merchants complained of a diminution in the consumption of Spanish wines. I was informed at Tepic of a measure precisely similar having been a few years earlier carried into effect in New Galicia, in the case of some extensive and flourishing tobacco plantations. The Americans were prevented, under severe penalties, from raising flax, hemp, or saffron. The culture of the grape and olive were forbidden, as Spain was understood to supply the colonies with wine and oil'. Tobacco, salt, gunpowder and quicksilver (used in extracting precious metals from the ore) were government monopolies; and to crown the colonists' grievances, the detested *alcavala*, a kind of purchase tax, was levied upon every transfer of goods.

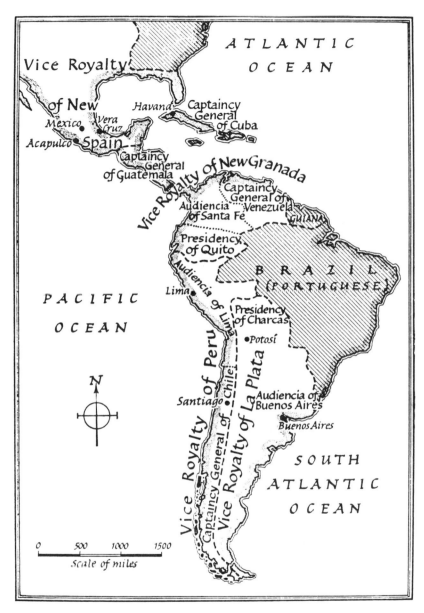

The viceroyalties and other
Spanish administrative
divisions.

THE NEW CONQUISTADORS

Although unable to meet the growing demands of the colonists for manufactured goods, the Spaniards spared no efforts to enforce a rigid monopoly of overseas trade with metropolitan Spain or its possessions. Until 1777 the port of Buenos Aires was in fact closed to all shipping, and imports to the colony were transported overland from Peru at vastly enhanced expense. 'No South American', as Captain Hall reports, 'could own a ship, nor could a cargo be consigned to him; no foreigner was allowed to reside in the country, unless born in Spain; and no capital, not Spanish, was permitted in any shape to be employed in the colonies. Orders were given, that no foreign vessel, on any pretence whatever, should touch a South American port. Even ships in distress were not to be received with common hospitality, but were ordered to be seized as prizes, and the crews imprisoned.'

It was the very rigidity of the Spanish embargo which resulted first in widespread smuggling and later, as the cause of independence gathered way, in a veritable army of foreign volunteers enlisting in the service of the emergent republics; and Captain Hall continues that: 'The South Americans, not withstanding the net-work of chains by which they were enveloped . . . longed earnestly for the enjoyments suitable to their nature; and finding that the Spaniards could nor would furnish them with an adequate supply, they invited the assistance of other nations. To this call the other nations were not slow to listen; and, in process of time, there was established one of the most extraordinary systems of organized smuggling which the world ever saw. This was known under the name of contraband or forced trade, and was carried out in armed vessels, well manned, and prepared to fight their way to the coast, and to resist, as they often did with effect, the guarda costas, or coast blockades of Spain. This singular system of warlike commerce was conducted by the Dutch, Portuguese, French, English, and latterly by the North Americans . . .

'How long it might have been before this . . . confined degree of intercourse with foreigners, if unaided by other causes, would have stimulated the Americans to assert their birthright, it is very difficult to say. Unforeseen circumstances, however, brought about that catastrophe, in some respects perhaps premature, which has recently broken their chains . . .'

The 'catastrophe' was the Peninsular War, which, by demonstrating the military and political impotence of Spain and Portugal, set the colonists on a course that stopped short of nothing but complete independence.

Revolutions are born in the hearts and minds of men, and most of the young creoles who were to spearhead the revolt were the sons of rich landowners and merchants in a position to visit Paris and London and to study in more depth the books by Voltaire, Raynal, Rousseau and Montesquieu, brought into South America by the contrabandists and periodically burnt by the censor. From Raynal they learned of Europe's mistakes in America; from Rousseau that government should be based upon the consent of the governed; and from Montesquieu, that 'The Indies and Spain are two powers under one master, but the Indies are the more important . . . Politics seek in vain to subordinate the more important to the less.'

Revolution broke out first in British North America and then in France, and the creoles saw words translated into action. Had it not been that they were much outnumbered by the underprivileged Indians, negroes and half-castes of doubtful allegiance, they might well have rebelled earlier. As it was, the execution of Louis XVI in France, the outbreak of the Terror and Napoleon's imperialistic designs in Europe gave them further cause for hesitation. Certainly the creoles were in no mind to exchange Spanish domination for French, so that their first steps towards independence were tentative.

When the *porteños*, or inhabitants of Buenos Aires, sensed their own strength, their first move was to set up in 1810 a 'Provisional Junta of the Provinces of the Rio de la Plata, governing for Ferdinand VII'; and other emergent nations followed the same course. Ferdinand, the 'Desired One', who had been bullied by Napoleon into abdicating the Spanish throne on the eve of the Peninsular War, did not respond to the colonists' overtures, once released from his prison in France. In 1812, Ferdinand had been compelled by *force majeure* to sign a liberal constitution, making certain concessions to his overseas subjects; but in 1820, when the Spanish empire had all but slipped from his grasp, he saw fit to declare:

> Americans, who find yourselves wandering far from the path
> that leads to prosperity, you now have what for so long you
> have been seeking at the cost of enormous efforts of ceaseless
> suffering, of bloody war, of awful desolation and of
> widespread destruction . . . So what are you waiting for?
> Harken to the gentle voice of your King and father . . .

Unfortunately, the Constitution of 1812, scornfully rejected by the reactionary Ferdinand on his first return to Spain and upon which he belatedly based his appeal to the colonists in 1820, was long ago a dead letter with the South Americans. Drawn up during the darkest days of the French invasion by an embattled Cortes, which had found a last refuge in beleaguered Cadiz, it was, as regards metropolitan Spain, an enlightened declaration of intent. By granting the colonists the same freedoms as Spaniards at home, the Cortes felt that it had removed legitimate grounds for revolt; but the Constitution did nothing to meet the demands for free trade with Europe and North America, so that the British envoy in Cadiz, Henry Wellesley, could report to Lord Castlereagh in July 1812: 'No disposition exists here to make any commercial concessions, even for the important object of tranquilizing America.' The somewhat niggardly restrictions on the number of American delegates to the Cortes – most of whom were in any case stand-ins from Cadiz – still further alienated the colonists.

A decade later Portugal adopted a Constitution modelled almost word for word on the Spanish example. Like the Cadiz Cortes, the Lisbon Junta of 1820 was liberal in its policies at home, but a similar obstinacy over the opening of Brazilian ports to foreign commerce led to the final rupture with the mother country.

From the times of Drake and Ralegh, the English, if it were possible, were no less obsessed with the gold of South America than the Spanish. Ralegh, in particular, was dazzled by the legend of El Dorado and between 1595 and 1618 mounted no less than four expeditions to explore the headwaters of the Orinoco and to discover the fabled city of Manoa. All resulted in failure and conflict with the Spanish. Having quarrelled with King James I of England, he obtained his release from the Tower in 1615 on the strength of promises for the exploitation of a great gold mine in Guiana. He lost both his fortune and his son in the attempt and paid for his ill-success with his head.

The legend of El Dorado died hard; but during the seventeenth and eighteenth centuries buccaneers and privateers, such as Henry Morgan, William Dampier, Thomas Braum and scores more, found it simpler and more profitable to let the Spanish produce the bullion and to prey on their galleons or raid their settlements along the Atlantic and Pacific coasts. The island of Juan Fernandez off the Chilean coast became a regular haven for such pirates; and Alexander Selkirk, a Scot from Largo in Fife, who was marooned there for four years, inspired Daniel Defoe to write *Robinson Crusoe*.

During the eighteenth century, when England and Spain were intermittently at war, the raids on shipping and ports were undertaken with the resources of the Royal Navy. The appearance of an

English sea-captain before the House of Commons, carrying one of his ears in cotton, and his allegation that the Spanish had accused him of smuggling and cut it off, provoked the War of Jenkin's Ear and the expeditions of Lord Anson and Admiral Vernon in 1740–1. After the Seven Years' War of 1756–63, Charles III of Spain entered into a 'family compact' between the Bourbon houses of Spain and France, giving comfort to the rebellious British colonists in North America and supporting their aspirations for independence. The toll on Spanish commerce continued during the decades before the outbreak of the Peninsular War, when the near-imbecile Charles IV left the conduct of foreign affairs to Manuel Godoy, 'The Prince of Peace', who veered disastrously between alliance with England and the propitiation of the all-conquering Napoleon. Until England entered the war in 1808 on the Spanish side, the British flag was therefore feared and hated rather than welcome in South American waters.

By then there had, in any case, been a significant change in attitude, both on the part of the South Americans and the British. As Napoleon occupied one European country after another, imposing a rigid blockade on imports from his arch-opponent, it became essential for Britain to seek alternative markets for the growing volume of goods produced in her new factories. The contraband trade, conducted largely from the safe base of a friendly Portuguese-controlled Brazil, had reached such proportions as to outweigh the proceeds of haphazard raids on Spanish shipping. Britain's first priority was therefore to regularize the position. On their side, the South American colonists realized that Spain and Portugal were no longer able to supply their needs nor to police the sea-lanes. Again, only Britain could guarantee Latin America against a French invasion.

One last and ill-judged fling to achieve El Dorado by brute force was to delay the moment when the spiritual descendants of the buccaneers and pirates were welcomed as liberators.

I The STRATEGY OF DELAY

ON 8 June, 1806, a British naval flotilla sailed into the estuary of the River Plate. Its materialization out of the empty South Atlantic was as much a surprise to the Spanish authorities in Buenos Aires as to the British government, when news of the operation reached London months later. But its commodore, Admiral Sir Home Rigg Popham, was an ambitious and unpredictable man; he was also under pressure from his creditors.

Having attacked and occupied the Dutch colony of the Cape of Good Hope according to instructions, he wearied of his routine patrol duties; and his thoughts turned to the easy pickings of South America. The commanding officer at the Cape lent him the 71st Regiment under Colonel Beresford (later and more honourably to reorganize the Portuguese army under Wellington); en route for Montevideo, he persuaded the Governor of St. Helena to lend him another four hundred men; and on receipt of news that a large consignment of specie had recently arrived in Buenos Aires from Peru, he determined to attack the city forthwith.

The Spanish Viceroy, Rafael de Sobremonte, was sitting in his box at the theatre, when, on 24 June, a messenger burst in with the news that the English were landing at Quilmes, south of the city. Sobremonte's first concern was to send away the treasure in bullock carts and he then gave orders for the approaches to be defended by the 3000 men at his disposal. Beresford brushed aside the resistance with a mixed force of 1635 Highlanders, marines and blue-jackets; the viceroy decamped with his family; and on 27 June the Union Jack was hoisted over the fort, where the Spanish flag had first been flown in the same month of June two hundred and twenty-six years before.

On 6 July Sir Home penned a despatch to the Admiralty to announce the capture of the city and further wrote to the Master of Lloyd's Coffee-house that 'the conquest of this place opens an extensive channel for the manufactures of Great Britain'. Meanwhile Beresford laid hands on treasure to the tune of 1,438,514 dollars (about £300,000 sterling), of which part was retained for the needs of the forces and the balance of 1,086,208 dollars sent to England in the frigate *Narcissus*. At first the *porteños* seemed resigned to the capture of their city, their commander, General Belgrano, even remarking: 'It grieved me to see my country subjugated in this manner, but I shall always admire the gallantry of the brave and honourable Beresford in so daring an enterprise.' However, the Americans were in no mind to exchange Spanish repression for the sovereignty of George III; and the invaders did not placate them simply by lowering the duties on British goods and proclaiming free trade.

Under the leadership of Juan Martín Puyrredón and Santiago Liniers, a Frenchman in the Spanish service, the citizenry began drilling in secret. A premature uprising under Puyrredón was summarily quelled; but on 12 August Liniers, who had received reinforcements from the Governor of Montevideo, entered Buenos Aires with an army of 4000. Beresford, who had sent home half of his Marine Battalion with the treasure, was driven back on the fort and, after fierce hand-to-hand fighting, compelled to surrender. The 1200 British soldiers were sent away in detachments to the interior. Although they had been promised repatriation to England, many of them, according to Michael Mulhall, 'married natives, and among their descendants are Senators, Deputies and Governors of the present time'. When General San Martín later formed his Army of the Andes for the liberation of Chile, he raised a battalion of *Cazadores Ingleses* from the British residents of the town of Mendoza, some of them ex-prisoners from Popham's expedition.*

Beresford and his senior officers were treated with great civility and whiled away their captivity with hunting and shooting parties. After five months in detention he and a Colonel Pack made contact with the Spanish Freemasons of the new lodge in Buenos Aires and were spirited on to a schooner for Montevideo – the Masons receiving life pensions of £300 a year from a grateful British government.

Years later, in 1825, when General William Miller was returning to Buenos Aires fresh from his triumphs in Peru, he recorded an incident which reflects the high respect of the Buenos Aireans for Beresford and his men. At dinner in Santiago de Estero on the northern borders of La Plata, 'the governor professed the utmost partiality towards Englishmen. He said he had two men in his escort who formerly belonged to the English army, who were faithful fellows, and who could ride like *gauchos*, but were a little given

---

* Mendoza has other links with England, one of the strangest being that, after his marriage to Queen Mary of England, Philip II of Spain named the region Nueva Inglaterra.

to tippling. General Beresford's name was often mentioned on this line of road. The natives inquired particularly if *"el guapo* Beresfor" was still living. They all concurred in acknowledging that he first taught them to be soldiers, and asked many questions as to his career after he had left that country.'

Popham, who had perforce witnessed the recapture of Buenos Aires from his ship, had meanwhile received substantial reinforcements from the Cape of Good Hope and attempted to revenge himself by the capture of Montevideo. The city fell to the British on 6 February, 1807 – but by this time Sir Home had been recalled to London to face court martial for embroiling the country in a war of his own making.

Popham's decision to attack Buenos Aires was not entirely unpremeditated. In 1784 there had arrived in London a Venezuelan exile, whose ceaseless intrigues for a revolution in South America during the next decades were to earn him the posthumous title of *El Precursor*. Francisco de Miranda was born of well-to-do parents in Caracas in 1750. After attending university, he left the country to serve with the Spanish army in Morocco. Thereafter, he fell out with his commanding officer, paid an extended visit to the United States and entered into correspondence with malcontents in Venezuela, including Juan V. Bolívar, whose son, Simón, was later to be known as 'The Liberator' and to become the most famous of the revolutionary leaders. Miranda was not altogether impressed by the Fathers of the North American revolution and, although originally hostile to England, came round to the opinion that, if South America was to be liberated, it must be with British help. On the first of his many visits to London he founded the *Gran Reunión Americana*, a society which was later to number many creole patriots, including the future Supreme Director of an independent Chile, Bernardo O'Higgins.

Miranda was warmly received by the British government under William Pitt the Younger, for whom access to the markets of South America was becoming an issue of increasing importance. In 1790, at the height of a dispute with Spain over trading rights with what is now British Columbia, it even seemed that Pitt might back his plans for an attack on Venezuela. But the years went by without the government committing itself – a pension of £300 a year was little consolation to the fiery Miranda – and in 1803 he won over Sir Home Popham, then seeking an outlet for his undoubted talents. Together, they presented an ambitious plan for an attack in the Caribbean. Once again it fell to the ground; but when Sir Home departed for the Cape in 1805, the scheme was still very much on his mind. He was later to maintain at his court martial that on taking leave of Pitt on 29 July:

> I had a long conversation with him on the original project of the expedition to South America; in the course of which Mr. Pitt informed me, that from the then state of Europe, and the confederation in part formed, and forming against France, there was a great anxiety to endeavour, by friendly negotiation, to detach Spain from her connection with that power; and, until the result of such an attempt should be known, it was desirable to suspend all hostile operations in South America; but, in case of failure in this object, it was his intention to enter on the original project.

It was before he heard of Pitt's death in January 1806 that Popham, without reference to the authorities in London, had set off from the Cape in April on his filibustering expedition. So deeply was Pitt's loss felt in England that his Tory government was succeeded by a coalition, the Ministry of All the Talents, formed both from Whigs of different shades of opinion, headed by Charles Fox and Lord Greville, and Tories under Lord Sidmouth. It greeted developments in South America with an agony of indecision. Sir Home Popham was at once recalled for court martial; but it was a year when Britain could show nothing to match Napoleon's triumphs on the Continent, and on the arrival of the treasure on 20 September, it was escorted through the streets to the Bank of England by excited crowds and bands playing 'God Save the King' and 'Rule Britannia'. The new Prime Minister, Lord Grenville, then decided to wash his hands of Europe. In ignorance of Beresford's subsequent débâcle, Sir Samuel Auchmuty was forthwith despatched to Buenos Aires with 3000 reinforcements; Sir Arthur Wellesley (the future Duke of Wellington) newly returned from India, was instructed to draw up plans for a general onslaught; and the talk was of nothing but the invasion and colonization of South America.

The bubble burst on 28 January, 1807, when news of Beresford's surrender at last reached London. In the meantime there had been dissenting voices in Parliament: Lord Holland and Lord Castlereagh, in particular, were sceptical about the government's plans. Was the navy equal to the task, and was the intention to enter South America as liberators or plunderers? The hard-headed Wellesley commented that 'every day affords a slighter hope that we shall be able to carry our plans into execution'. The Ministry of All the Talents resigned itself to restoring British prestige and, having hastily assembled and despatched a relief expedition under General Whitelocke, shortly afterwards collapsed.

Thus far the British incursion into the Plate had been a comedy of errors; the sequel in South America fell little short of farce – and as every writer of farce is aware, his victim must first side step the banana skin before slipping on it.

On 5 January, 1807, Rear-Admiral Stirling arrived with Auchmuty to supersede Sir Home Popham. The two continued the attack on Montevideo to such purpose that they routed the garrison of 6000 and occupied the city on 6 February. In May they were themselves superseded by General Whitelocke, whose 5000 troops brought the invasion force to 10,000. Repeating the tactics successfully used by Beresford twelve months before, Whitelocke toiled through the swamps to Quilmes, then forced back an army of 6000 under Liniers to the approaches of Buenos Aires, where a counter-attack was decisively repulsed by troops under Generals Levison Gower and Crawfurd. So sharp was his reverse that Liniers now urged the *Cabildo* (or city council) to surrender; but Whitelocke was unaccountably held back for a couple of days, which the *Cabildo* put to good use in setting up barricades and batteries.

When, on the morning of 5 July, 1807, the attacking column entered the town, 'The British troops,' as General Mitre wrote later, 'worthy of a better General, marched resolutely to their sacrifice, advancing as fearlessly as on parade along those avenues of death, enfiladed at right angles every 150 yards: Whitelocke remaining with the reserve at the Miserere, entirely cut off from the rest of his army. The result of such tactics could not but prove disastrous.' By nightfall 2,200 men had been killed, wounded or taken prisoner; and on the following day Whitelocke ignominiously surrendered and agreed to evacuate the province within ten days, and Montevideo in two months.

Whitelocke returned to England to be court martialled and dismissed the service. Mulhall adds that 'it was generally believed he would have been shot but that he was supposed to be a natural son of a member of the royal family'; and for years afterwards there was a common toast in English taverns: 'Success to grey hairs, but bad luck to white locks.'

Ironically enough, the ill-fated Whitelocke probably achieved more for England by losing than by winning. The British troops had behaved well, so that on the evacuation of Montevideo the *Cabildo* actually presented their commander with a valedictory address:

> We should be unworthy of the name of men were we not to
> acknowledge our gratitude, and to tender our warmest
> thanks to you and Sir S. Auchmuty for your generosity and
> ceaseless exertions to lessen our sufferings, and alleviate the
> miseries of war. Families were treated with the utmost
> tenderness and respect. The pride of victorious troops who
> had just conquered a city, and entered through fire and
> blood, was in a moment suppressed, and their exultation
> reduced to quiet and tranquillity. Such recollections will
> render the memory of Sir S. Auchmuty and yourself dear to
> us, and we shall ever pray that every happiness which your
> exalted virtue deserves may attend your steps.

The *porteños* emerged from the scuffle with enhanced self-
confidence, since it had been a citizen army, rather than Spanish
regulars, which had repulsed the invaders. They had briefly
enjoyed the benefits of free trade; and when Liniers, the hero of the
hour, was appointed acting Viceroy, he not only winked at the
continuing presence of British traders, but took no action to check
the growing market in contraband. Matters were taken a step
further when in September 1809 a young creole lawyer, Mariano
Moreno, published a tract openly advocating free trade, in direct
opposition to the official policy of a Spanish monopoly. The new
Viceroy, who had meanwhile replaced Liniers, was compelled to
climb down to the extent of permitting a limited free trade with
nations friendly to Spain; and this paved the way, first for the
creation of the 'Provisional Junta of the Provinces of the Río de la
Plata, governing for Ferdinand VII' in May 1810 and for the outright
declaration of independence in 1816.

Although Popham's bold irruption on the South American scene
hastened independence – in a way unforeseen by its instigator – it
was entirely out of step with British foreign policy, which was
characterized by caution and diplomatic manoeuvring, until Canning deemed the time ripe to grant recognition to Colombia and
Mexico in 1825. As long ago as the seventeenth century, faced with
the colonists' demands for manufactured goods which she could
not herself supply, Spain had permitted their import via Cadiz and
Seville, whence they were transported in Spanish vessels. Britain
participated in this indirect trade and as part of the fruits of the
Treaty of Utrecht in 1713 had obtained the *Asiento* or contract to
supply slaves to South America. The operations of the South Sea
Company, formed for the purpose, provided a cloak for a huge and
lucrative contraband trade in English goods; and even after the

Asiento was surrendered in 1750, the Spanish were unable to put a stop to it.

As Napoleon extended his stranglehold over continental Europe during the first years of the nineteenth century, the need to find an alternative market for the cotton and woollen goods, the iron and the china produced in ever-increasing amounts in England's new factories, became imperative. Hence even Pitt, obsessed with his scheme for building up an effective opposition to Napoleon in the shape of an alliance with Russia, Austria and Sweden, the so-called Third Coalition, turned aside to dally with Miranda. By 1807 a new Secretary of State of War, Castlereagh, had decided that the only means of breaking the Spanish monopoly was his scheme for armed intervention on behalf of the dissident colonists, for which Wellesley, although not much impressed by the volatile Miranda, had now made definite plans.

Within months, British policy underwent an abrupt volte-face; Napoleon's armies had invaded Spain, and Canning was pledging British support to a delegation from the Supreme Junta of the Asturias. Clearly His Britannic Majesty could not ally himself to Spain in the struggle against Napoleon and at the same time foment rebellion in her colonies. It was the plain-spoken Sir Arthur Wellesley, shortly to enbark his troops for the Peninsula instead of South America, who was given the painful task of disillusioning Miranda:

> I think I never had a more difficult business, than when the
> Government bade me tell Miranda that we would have
> nothing to do with his plan. I thought it best to walk out in
> the streets with him and tell him there, to prevent his
> bursting out. But even there he was so loud and angry, that I
> told him I would walk on first a little that we might not
> attract the notice of everybody passing. When I joined him
> again he was cooler. He said: 'You are going over into Spain
> (this was before Vimiero) – you will be lost – nothing can
> save you; that, however, is your affair; but what grieves me
> is that there never was such an opportunity thrown away!'

In the face of Spanish disasters in the field and the need to re-equip their defeated armies from England, and with the British troops hard-pressed to maintain a toe-hold in the Peninsula, it was not long before Canning's thoughts returned to the freeing of trade with South America. He wrote to Sir Arthur's brother, the Marquess of Wellesley, envoy to the Seville Junta:

. . . it is obvious that if Spain were desirous of making a
return for the assistance and protection which she has
received, such return was to be found, not in mere phrases
and professions and empty promises of impracticable and
unnecessary aid to Great Britain, but in exertions and
sacrifices of another and more practicable kind . . . in
opening to British commerce the ports of Spanish America,
and thereby enabling this country to recruit the stock of
specie which has been exhausted in the service of Spain.

Secure in the knowledge that Britain was far too involved to withdraw from the Peninsula, the Junta turned a deaf ear to the pleas
and protests alike; and in July 1810 the visit to London of two
Venezuelan agents, Simón Bolívar and Luis López Méndez, began
a new chapter in British policy towards South America. The envoys
launched into an impassioned appeal for British intervention in
Venezuela; the Marquess of Wellesley, who had succeeded Canning as Foreign Minister, gave them a sympathetic hearing, but
would commit himself no further than a promise of naval support in
the event of a French attack and the offer of his services as mediator
in settling the differences with the mother country. The Marquess,
like his successors at the Foreign Office, found himself on a tight-
rope. Britain's longterm interests lay in regularizing and expanding
her trade with South America; she could not afford to offend the
colonists, nor, on the other hand, could she contemplate an open
breach with Spain that would still further lengthen the odds against
Wellington in the Peninsula.

The solution was a typical British compromise. The Spaniards,
while utterly opposed to legalizing trade with their colonies, were
resigned to the entry of contraband, which, with their depleted
military and naval resources, they were in any case powerless to
stop. An opportunity for augmenting the flow of goods came with
the French occupation of Lisbon and the flight of the Portuguese
royal family to Brazil in November 1807. Lord Strangford, who had
provided a naval escort for the fugitives, himself arrived in Rio de
Janeiro on 22 July, 1808, with instructions 'to make the Brazils an
emporium for British manufactures destined for the whole of South
America'. The Prince Regent of Brazil, Don Pedro, had already
opened the country's ports for trade with friendly nations and in
February 1810 signed a far-reaching Treaty of Commerce and
Navigation between Brazil and Britain. The immediate result was a
positive avalanche of British manufactured goods, including such
unlikely items as chandeliers, warming pans, ice skates and
hatchets – supplied by a romantic, if uninformed manufacturer – for
chipping gold from the living rock. By 1812, when the furore had

subsided and trade had been organized on a more sensible basis, it was estimated that the larger part of these exports found their way from Brazil to Spanish America.

Britain's readiness and ability to supply the needs of the Spanish colonists won her a fund of goodwill and impressed the leaders of the emergent republics far more than revolutionary propaganda from France or expressions of sympathy from the United States. As one after another of the colonies won independence, the customs duties on British imports became a main source of revenue for their juntas. (Thus, when Lord Cochrane, with his family and entourage took ship in the *Rose* and arrived in Valparaiso to assume command of the Chilean navy, a needy government reimbursed her captain by waiving £2000 payable in dues on her cargo.) Additional large funds found their way into the exchequers of the new regimes – such as the £1 million loan floated in London and advanced to Chile in 1822, when she was still fighting for her own independence and Peru's – so that Lord Palmerston could later report to Parliament that no less than £150 million sterling had been lent in South America. And, although successive Spanish legates in London made bitter complaints about the provision of equipment and arms to the insurgents, ways and means were found of welcoming revolutionary agents and quietly meeting their requirements.

The successful conclusion of the Peninsular War in 1814 brought no dramatic change in British foreign policy; and neither Castlereagh nor Canning yielded to the increasing pressure for outright recognition of the new states until by 1825 matters had reached a point of no return. The reason was no longer the fear of antagonizing a largely impotent Spain, but rather to avoid giving pretext to the reactionary Ferdinand VII, now restored to the throne, for seeking the aid of one of Britain's partners of the Grand Alliance in re-establishing Spanish rule in America. Britain, by backstage means and the unobtrusive deployment of the navy, had assumed a predominant role in South America and was in no way disposed to share it or to countenance intervention by Russia or her other European allies. To Ferdinand's increasingly urgent appeals for British help in restoring the worsening position in America, Castlereagh, and Canning after him, returned the bland answer that Britain was prepared to mediate – but only on condition that Spain granted free trade. As this was totally unacceptable, both to Ferdinand and the merchants of Seville and Cadiz, all the successive negotiations fell to the ground.

After Castlereagh's suicide in 1822, Canning was increasingly preoccupied with the possibility of armed intervention by France, and in October 1823 set the seal to his intricate policy of playing off one power against another by inducing the French ambassador in London, the Prince de Polignac, to agree to a memorandum pledging France not to intervene 'by force or by menace' in South America. The so-called Polignac memorandum, by removing any effective threat from Europe, largely stole the thunder from the United States when President Monroe shortly afterwards spelt out his famous Doctrine, warning the rest of the world against intervention in the American hemisphere.

Britain's ability to help the South Americans achieve independence was made possible by the ubiquitous presence of what an American writer, William W. Kaufmann, has called 'that most discreet of all military engines' – the Royal Navy. First and foremost it provided the colonists with a shield against outside interference from France. It also facilitated the commerce which was the life blood of revolution. During the period 1810–25, which saw the transformation of two great colonial empires into independent republics, Spanish susceptibilities prevented the British government from appointing official diplomatic representatives. But, as has been well put by Gerald S. Graham and R. A. Humphreys in *The Navy and South America*, 'though it was impossible that Britain should enter into formal relations with such revolutionary authorities, the Admiralty correspondence affords ample evidence of British success in maintaining informal relations by means of amphibious plenipotentiaries on the South American station . . .

'For long periods the captains of His Majesty's ships faced successive waves of political tension almost without parallel in the history of British naval diplomacy . . . Patriot privateers, with or without letters of marque, attacked and ransacked neutral ships on the plea that Spanish contraband was on board or that paper blockades had been infringed; Spanish vessels of war took prizes without enquiring too carefully into national origins, and when these so-called prizes were brought to port, uncomfortable detentions often ensued, sometimes confiscations, and long-drawn-out appeals. Privateers, moreover, sometimes turned pirates, and at every port the temptation to honest traders to become smugglers was almost irresistible . . . In these circumstances the greatest patience, forebearance and statesmanship were vital, and naval commanders like William Bowles and Thomas Masterman Hardy had to restrain their talents for pugnacious action in the interests of diplomacy and trade . . .'

While Castlereagh and Canning indulged a taste for the subtleties of power politics and the Navy did its scrupulous best to hold the ring, there were Britains, who, either out of idealism or for plain gain, were forthright in their support of the rebellious colonists and were prepared to risk life and limb in the struggle for independence. With the end of the Peninsular War and the North American campaign of 1812–14, thousands of soldiers and sailors found themselves without employment or on half-pay. The emergent republics were eager for their services, particularly in forming navies to challenge the Spanish at sea. Thousands of disbanded soldiers were recruited in England and Ireland for Bolívar's British Legions; talented officers like Lord Cochrane and William Miller came forward with individual offers of service; and H.M. brig *Hecate* was actually bought from the Navy by her commander and commissioned fully armed and manned.

The Navy's attitude towards such individual enterprise was generally disapproving, as emerges vividly from a despatch of Bowles, then Commodore of the South American station, to John Croker, the Secretary of the Admiralty, from Buenos Aires in December 1818:

> It is not difficult to see that the class of foreigners entrusted with the principal naval commands are as likely to use their power and influence for the gratification of their private interests or feelings as for the advantage of the country which employs them. Their Lordships will judge what sort of conduct may be expected from Lord Cochrane . . .

The Commodore also waxed indignant on the mass desertions of merchant seamen and even their own ratings to the navies of the republics, which at the time of Admiral Brown's onslaught on the Brazilian navy in 1825–6 had reached such proportions that the Brazilian navy alone numbered 1200 British sailors.

In deference to heated protests from Spain and Portugal, Britain's Prince Regent in 1817 delivered a stern warning to his subjects not to participate in foreign revolutions – with such small effect that in 1818 Colonel English enlisted some 1200 volunteers at £50 a head for service in Venezuela, and 'General' Devereux rather later set up his headquarters at a Dublin hotel and openly recruited a further 2000 Irish volunteers for Bolívar's armies. In May 1819 the Government, in the face of violent opposition, forced a Foreign Enlistment Act through the Commons, which debarred British subjects from entering the service of any foreign nation. Its provisions were never enforced with any rigour. Lord Cochrane, the most famous volunteer of all, escaped prosecution when he returned to England in

1825, after his destruction of the Spanish and Portuguese navies in Chilean, Peruvian and Brazilian waters had made him a household name.

John Taylor, later to become one of Cochrane's ablest lieutenants, was the subject of a strong complaint from Sir Thomas Hardy to the Admiralty in February 1823 after his defection to the Brazilians from the frigate *Blossom*. The Admiralty minuted a stern rejoinder, noting that 'the profferr'd resignation of Mr. Taylor is obviously a mere pretence' and instructing Hardy 'to avail himself of any occasion that may offer, without violating the Brazilian territory or flag, of seeking the deserter and either bringing him home to trial before a court martial on the station or sending him with sufficient witnesses home to be tried in England'.

Taylor was, in fact, never brought to book and ended a distinguished career as an admiral of the Brazilian navy; and the conclusion must be that the Foreign Enlistment Act was passed merely *pro forma* and as a sop to Spain and Portugal.

It is perhaps understandable that naval commanders in South America, whose prime concern was to facilitate the short-term interests of British merchants in trading both with the rebels and the colonies still in Spanish hands, should deprecate the high-handed interference of a Cochrane or a Brown with neutral shipping. And, debarred from energetic or spectacular action themselves, they were not a little jealous of their freebooting compatriots. Thus, in May 1821, Hardy, in transmitting to the Admiralty a detailed list of the units of Cochrane's Chilean fleet and its British officers, ends rather plaintively: 'I beg to add that the whole duty of the squadron is carried out in the English language, and the uniform is as much like ours as possible . . .'

Both the Navy and the volunteers played a significant part in reshaping the map of South America; but, whatever the real sympathies of the government at home, the Navy had the difficult and unrewarding role of being seen to be impartial. Although ultimate independence had become inevitable, it was the more downright involvement of British soldiers and seamen that hastened it.

II The AMATEUR ADMIRAL

AMONG the early British settlers in Buenos Aires was William Brown, who, without previous naval experience, was to form a fleet for the young republic and to deploy it with such effect as to drive the Spanish navy from the waters of the Plate and later to thwart Brazil's expansionist ambitions in the area.

Shortly before his death in 1857 Brown committed to paper, in the form of 150 pages of holograph manuscript, the memoirs of his services in the cause of the Republic, sending them to the Minister of War, Bartolomé Mitre, with a letter in which he says: 'I wish to finish this work before undertaking the long journey towards the shadowy seas of death.' Mitre responded appropriately by writing that Brown could never be lost among the shadows, but must take his place among the shining immortals. The *Memorias* and an extensive collection of his letters and despatches throw a sharp light on his naval operations; but, as his Argentinean biographer, Héctor Ratto, has remarked, his origins and early career are obscure. Nevertheless, the journalistic, but usually reliable Michael Mulhall fills out the picture.

It seems that Brown was born on 22 June, 1777, at Foxford, County Mayo, the son of an Irish smallholder, and was educated by a Roman Catholic priest, a man of considerable culture, who had lived for a period in Spain. His father emigrated to the United States and died of yellow fever only a few days after his arrival, leaving the boy an orphan at the age of nine. A Philadelphia sea-captain offered the lad a job as cabin boy, and twenty years later, at the time of the Napoleonic wars, he had risen to the command of an English merchantman, which was captured by the French ship *Président*.

He was imprisoned, first at the fortress of Metz, from which he escaped in the dress of a French officer, and after his recapture, at Verdun. Here he occupied a cell above that of a Colonel Clutchwell and succeeded in tunnelling through and effecting their escape. After they had wandered for some days in the forest of Ardennes, living on dry chocolate, Clutchwell was so exhausted that Brown had to carry him to the banks of the Rhine, whence they made their way to Württemberg and appealed to the Grand Duchess. An English princess, she helped the couple to make their way home, where Brown married a Miss Chitty, to whom he remained devoted all his life.

He appears on the South American scene in 1809, when, basing himself on Montevideo, he began a coastal trade with Brazil. By 1810 he was captain and proprietor of the schooner *Jane* and established in Buenos Aires, where he was an eyewitness of the first acts of revolution. The following year he acquired a second ship, the *Eliza*, which ran aground; he was nevertheless able to salvage and sell the cargo. With the proceeds he bought the schooner *Industria* and in partnership with Pío White, later to become quartermaster of the Republican fleet, established the first packet service between Buenos Aires and La Colonia, upstream on the Plate from Montevideo (see map, page 129). This was brought to an end by the Spanish navy's arbitrary seizure of the ship, an act which Brown never forgave the authorities in Montevideo and which no doubt disposed him to take up arms on behalf of the revolutionary government of Buenos Aires.

Relations between La Plata and the royalists of the Banda Oriental, the territory bordering the Uruguay river, of which Montevideo was the capital, had been strained since the creation of the Provisional Junta in Buenos Aires in 1810. The situation was complicated by the rival claims to the Banda Oriental of Portugal and of the fiercely nationalistic José Artigas, one of that 'sort of Christian savages called Gauchos,' as Sir Walter Scott wrote, 'whose principal furniture is the skulls of horses, whose only food is raw beef and water . . . and whose chief amusement is to ride wild horses to death. Unhappily they were found to prefer their national independence to cottons and muslins.'

Matters were aggravated by the proposal of the notorious Princess Carlota, the Spanish-born wife of Dom John of Portugal, a refugee in Brazil since the French coup of 1807, to establish a regency over the whole of Spanish South America after the imprisonment of her brother, Ferdinand VII, in France. The Princess was described by Madame Junot, later Duchess of Abrantes, in her *Memoirs*, as 'a woman four feet ten inches high at the very most, and crooked, or at least both her sides were not alike; her bust, arms, and legs, being in perfect unison with her deformed shape' – and her morals were in keeping with her appearance.

Unfortunately, Sir Sidney Smith, commander of the Royal Navy's South American station, was injudicious enough to support her; and it required his recall to London and all the diplomatic gifts of

Lord Strangford, the British envoy to Rio de Janeiro, to restore the uneasy *status quo*. Strangford was of opinion that it would best benefit Britain to allow the colonists to work out their own salvation; for seven years he strove to maintain peace of a sort; but after his return to London, the Junta in Buenos Aires decided upon an outright attack on their royalist compatriots across the Plate in January 1814.

On 22 January Brown was writing to John Larrea of the Buenos Aires Junta:

> Excellent Sir,
>   I beg to inform your Excellency that in consequence of reports being spread abroad, as to my becoming a fighting man & which has reached the ears of an affectionate wife, far advanced in a state of pregnancy, I must decline having the pleasure of serving you, the peace and tears of my family requires it. Men as capable, if not more so, can be had in Buenos Aires . . .

This was not the opinion of the government. Although Brown was a merchant seaman, it seems that during the twenty unrecorded years on the high seas he must have seen a great deal of naval warfare, at any rate from the sidelines; and more recently his ships had been involved in armed conflict with the Spanish. A reference to one of his vessels in the same letter is evidence of his familiarity with naval matters:

> Her crew will always be at the disposal of your service. Should she be fortunate in taking prizes, it will be the means of encouraging the well manning of others. Three complete Signal books well adopted, similar to that of the British Navy, I will make, to the end that vessels may converse in sight of their spy-glasses . . .

But Larrea had decided that Brown, who enjoyed the reflected glory of Nelson and Rodney, was his man. Since the Junta possessed no warships, a squadron of three small vessels was fitted out, comprising the *Hercules*, an old Russian trader of 350 tons; the *Zephyr*, an English brig of 220 tons; and the schooner *Nancy*. In February 1814 Brown was appointed Commodore with the rank of lieutenant-colonel and hoisted his flag in the *Hercules*. It was, however, only after a heated dispute with Captain Seaver, who had joined the flotilla with his seven-gun schooner *Julieta*, that he gained undisputed command and proceeded to attack the off-shore island of Martín García near Colonia. The Spanish admiral, Romarate, was

Ferdinand VII of Spain, 'The Desired One'.

Left Portrait of Sir Arthur Wellesley, later 1st Duke of Wellington.

Right Admiral William Brown.

George Canning.

Above Gaucho balling an ostrich.

Above Gaucho soldier.

Below A gaucho killing a puma with his *bolas*.

lying in wait beneath guns of the shore batteries, and a lucky shot killed the *Hercules'* pilot and caused the ship to run aground; Captain Seaver was killed simultaneously; and the other patriot vessels retreated, leaving the flagship to fight it out alone. By morning, when the tide floated her off, Brown had lost half of the ship's company of 200, including her captain, Elias Smith. Of this first encounter he was subsequently to send a biting report to Larrea:

> Appropos you talk of cooperation, and permit me to ask you, Sir, if it can be imagined, that I would come here, did I know, that there would be none, pray Mr. Larrea can I make fighting men of damned cowards, my blood heats when I think of their cowardly behaviour at the moment when nothing was wanting but their bringing to an anchor. Some arrangement I disapproved of but the philosophising Mr. White, who I sincerely wish, was in my place, did as he thought proper. He Mr. W. would see his error, in giving commands to men, particularly who never saw a cannon, unless it war [were] at a distance and such men, am I to cooperate with. Enough. I trust nothing will be wanting, or I hope not, on my side, to make the gentlemen fight . . .

The *Hercules* had been hulled in eighty-two places, but was run aground near Colonia for hasty repairs with lead plugs and canvas steeped in tar. Resuming the attack on Martín García on 16 March, Brown landed 150 men under hot fire and overcame the Spanish garrison. Romarate, of whom Brown said that he never met a braver man, retreated up the Uruguay river, pursued by Captain Norther, whose ship ran aground and was blown up by her crew with the loss of all hands.

Brown returned to the attack in May with a larger squadron of seven ships, carrying 147 guns and 1252 men and almost exactly matched by the thirteen ships of his opponent, Admiral Sierra, with 155 cannon and 1180 men (Romarate still being bottled up in the Uruguay). Brown first succeeded in separating Sierra's flagship from the rest of his fleet, then in luring the remaining Spanish ships into deep water and interposing his own squadron between them and the shore. Next, in a manoeuvre reminiscent of Nelson's at Trafalgar, he divided the Spanish line, passing between the *San José* and the *Neptuno*, both of which were later captured, together with the *Paloma*. The crews of three further ships set fire to them and escaped ashore, while the remainder of the demoralized fleet dispersed in utter confusion. During an early exchange of fire Brown's leg was fractured by a cannon ball, obliging him to direct operations from a seat on deck.

Pursuing the last Spanish units into port, where the garrison was ringing the church bells for the anticipated victory, Brown dressed his ship in bunting and fired an ironical salute of twenty-one guns to signalize the destruction of the Spanish fleet, then returned to Buenos Aires, leaving his second-in-command, Oliver Russell, to blockade Montevideo, which was by now beleaguered by a *porteño* army under General Alvear.

After a round of celebrations and banquets in Buenos Aires, the victorious Brown, while still on crutches, had himself carried on board his flagship and set sail again for Montevideo, where he landed a large force under a Captain Kearney to reinforce the besieging army. The Spanish governor, General Vigodet, surrendered on 20 June, 1814. Brown proved to be a generous victor, entertaining him on board the *Hercules* until arrangements were made for his passage to Rio de Janeiro, en route for Spain, and further presenting him with thirty ounces of gold from his own pocket for the expense of the voyage.

Although Montevideo and the Banda Oriental were not destined to remain for long in the hands of the *porteños*, Brown had rendered Buenos Aires secure from any attempt by the Spanish navy; and his services were recognized by his promotion to Admiral in July 1814 and the presentation to him of the *Hercules* some months later. Far from resting on his laurels, he now conceived the bold plan of 'a cruize intended to be performed in the Pacific Sea against the Royalist Spaniards. Who not being satisfied with carrying on a destructive war [from Upper Peru], which has deluged with blood the United Provinces and Rio de la Plata since the 25th of May 1810, are again endeavouring to uphold with new effort, deeming to all the horrors of polluted conquest and rapacity, the innocent inhabitants of said provinces who durst judge for themselves in vindicating their rights as an independent people.'

The expedition was fitted out partly at his own expense and partly at that of the government; and on 15 September, 1815, he set sail for Cape Horn with the *Hercules*, carrying 200 men and 20 guns, and the *Trinidad*, commanded by his brother, Michael, with 16 guns and 130 men. They were shortly followed by two other small ships, the *Hawk*, under Captain Bouchard, and the new American-built schooner *Constitución*, renamed the *Uribe* in honour of the Chilean patriot who had contributed to fitting her out. Both Uribe and her captain, Oliver Russell, who had been Brown's second-in-command in the Plate, were drowned when the ship foundered off Cape Horn with the loss of all her hundred hands.

The *Hercules* and the *Trinidad* also encounted fearful weather after rounding the Horn and were separated. In Brown's own words, 'The gale continuing with heavy showers of sleet and snow about noon, a bay was discovered at no great distance upon the lee bow. Here a second anchor was let go, under the lee of a reef of rocks expecting that both anchors might bring the ship up, but no, she still kept driving and the wind blowing direct upon the land, there was not alternative left but to slip both iron chains, make sail and endeavour to beat out, and search for the Brig and companions, the fate of whom it was much feared was worse than those on board the *Hercules*. This however could not be accomplished, for not being able to weather a point of land at the foot of a stupendous mountain, the ship in the act of missing stays, gently struck the rocks and carried away a part of the cut water from the keel upwards. After receiving this blow she was with the help of a little sail, forced round a second point, but got on a sunken reef on which she lay thumping for about two hours, untill ropes were run out and fastened to the trees by which she was hove off.

'The people's anxiety to get on shore with the ships in this situation can hardly be described as every blow during the time of striking, theatened to send the masts over the bows. But as the boats were manned with best officers and seamen, no desertion took place, until she was hove into a dock formed by nature, where she lay as if alongside a wharf with a steep rock on the offside on which the seamen used to gather mussels at low water . . .

'After seven days stay for repairs in this gloomy place called Timor bay, where there was not a living creature to be seen, the elements forbidding by their intense cold even the existence of fish in the water except mussels, the guns etc., etc., were taken on board, the water compleated and the unfortunate deserters sought by all possible means, but all to no avail; and we sailed leaving six unhappy men either to die with hunger, or perish with cold, a fate that was lamented by every man on board. Had it not been for the precaution taken and the exemplary punishment of the sargent of Marines, a greater calamity would have taken place, probably to the amount of one half the crew. A little provisions, an axe, cooking pot, old sail, a fire and two blankets with two muskets and ammunition were left on shore for their use.'

To Brown's intense relief the *Hercules* succeeded in making rendezvous with the *Trinidad* and the *Hawk* near Mocha Island off the Chilean coast. The squadron then proceeded to cruise off Lima in Peru, where numbers of prizes were taken. Two attempts were made on its harbour of Callao, during one of which the Spanish corvette *Fuente Hermosa* was sunk under the guns of the shore batteries. After blockading the port for fourteen days, Brown sailed north to Guayaquil in search of supplies.

Acting on the information of a patriot officer from the army of New Granada (present-day Colombia), whom he had released from imprisonment on board one of the Spanish prizes, he sailed up the Guayaquil river in the *Trinidad* expecting a friendly reception, but was met by a hot fire from the forts ashore. Having silenced two of them, the *Trinidad* ran aground opposite the remaining battery. 'The boats crews on shore being under no command and made bold by the success of victory went absolutely into the town to get grog, in lieu of returning to their duty.' The Spaniards then rallied and raked the ship with such a destructive fire that Brown had no alternative but to strike his colours and to jump into the river 'surrounded by alligators' in the hopes of swimming to an accompanying schooner further down. Unable to reach her, he returned to the *Trinidad*.

'The scene that followed was horrid, the long and sharp knife being set to work on the throats and hearts of the miserable wounded . . . I laid hold of a cutlass on one hand with lighted match in the other and proceeded for the magazine, requesting as I went through the cabbin, the captain of the [captured] *Consequencia*, a prisoner on board, to go on deck and endeávour to save the lives (by putting an end to the cool blooded acts of murder that was then taking place) of my men, and inform the Governor . . . that Brown, the Commander in Chief of the patriotic expedition, was gone to the Magazin, with a determination of blowing the vessel, himself and every soul on board into the eléments, if he is not immediately with all his officers and men promised the treatment of prisoners of war on the word and honour of the Governor . . .'

On the Governor's complying, Brown then evacuated the magazine, 'Where I had nigh been blown up without committing the act myself; the desire of Plunder among all who boarded being so great that every locker was ransacked and the rabble becoming in a state of intoxication from the abundance of wine and spirits on board, that many were smocking their sigars among the loose powder and cartridges; and two men had actually droped their lighted sigars down the scuttle of the magazine upon a few empty flannel cartridges that lay upon barrels of gunpowder. And had it not been that a man who had just swam on board had jumped down the scuttle with his trousers dripping wet upon the sigars, the explosion must inevitably have taken place, so that the escape was truly miraculous. Such was, it is to be presumed the divine will of Providence . . .'

As well as being a very devout man, Brown was also scrupulously neat and tidy. It has been recorded that he insisted on his quarters being scoured with sand and washed with soap daily and that before going into action he donned full dress uniform. He was therefore doubly shocked to find his cabin ransacked and that, after his swim in the river, he had been left without even a pair of trousers. Going on deck and draping himself in a patriot flag, he made his way to the shore and was all but lynched under the eyes of the Governor, who had ridden to the beach to witness the scene.

The Governor nevertheless retrieved himself by issuing an invitation to dinner, accompanied by a clean suit of clothes. '"Come," he said, "and sit you down by me, for although you have given us something to do in the way of aiding our appetites, I am determined you shall dine with us, sin ceremonia."' The bishop, who sat on the Governor's other side, was equally suave: '"Why, you appear as easy and contented as if you were in Bs. As. and amongst your friends; perhaps you don't know into whose hands you have fallen. Or do you expect to escape from hence with your life?"' Brown replied with equal urbanity that '"if I was now to get rid of life in so tragical manner, I would first wish to have the pleasure of taking a glass of wine with His Reverence"' and was convinced that 'had I acted a servile or timid part, death must e'been [have been] my doom'.

He probably owed his release fourteen days later to the uncertainty of the royalist authorities as to the loyalty of the inhabitants, to whom the other prisoners 'explained the motive of the expedition as being entirely with a view to revolutionizing the town and putting it in the possession of the Patriots; which information as soon as communicated generally, had a good effect, all having declared that had such been known in time, there would not have been a single shot fired, the natives of Guayaquil being of opinion with their brethren of Bs. As., that the Americas should be free and entirely independent of Spain.' Meanwhile the *Hercules* and the *Hawk* proceeded up the river, and the Governor, yielding to *force majeure*, despatched a flag of truce and agreed to an exchange of prisoners and the payment of $22,000 for the return of a Spanish prize.

However, Brown's troubles were mounting. First, Captain

Bouchard insisted on returning to Buenos Aires and demanded one of the prizes, as the *Hawk* was leaking and in no condition to undertake the voyage. Brown then sailed north to the bay of Buenaventura; and attempts were made to repair the *Hawk*, which capsized, taking to the bottom with her a smaller vessel containing most of the squadron's provisions. The ship's surgeon, Dr Handford, had meanwhile been sent inland in search of supplies; but after six weeks it was learned that he had fallen ill of fever and that the royalist General Morillo was fast advancing to the coast.

The *Hercules*, now alone and leaking, and almost without provisions, steered for the Galapagos Islands, where a supply of seventy large turtles, weighing about 150 lbs. each, was taken on board. Weighing anchor on 20 June, 1816, she then headed south for the 10,000 mile return voyage to Buenos Aires, 'notwithstanding the shortness of allowances which amounted to one biscuit, a gill of Indian corn, a gill of rice, a pound of tortoise, half a pound of meat and a half pint of rum, per man per day, the which might be thought sufficient, and would, were not the men worked to such a degree, as some to fall to the deck with weakness occasioned by the fatigue of pumping . . .'

After rounding Cape Horn – not without scraping a large iceberg – the *Hercules* steered for the Falklands, but fell in with such bad weather that she had to continue towards Buenos Aires, 'trusting to Providence for an alleviation of thirst and hunger'. Soon afterwards Brown fell in with the brig *Fanny* homeward bound from Montevideo and was dismayed to learn that a Portuguese army of 10,000 was in the vicinity of the city and that a squadron from Rio de Janeiro was on its way to blockade the Plate. 'After receiving this information from the Brig with two bags of bread, it was resolved unanimously by every man on board, to look for some friendly port'; and on 25 September, 1816, the *Hercules* finally dropped anchor at Barbados. Here, Brown was to drain the cup of bitterness to the dregs.

A request to repair the ship was refused by the Governor, Sir J. Leith, in view of 'the circumstances under which the *Hercules* came into that port'. In spite of his permission to revictual her and to proceed to a free port, she was next seized by Captain James Stirling of H.M.S. *Brazen*, but released on the Governor's orders. Stirling then treacherously suggested that the two ships should sail in company to Antigua, where 'he was sure I would obtain permission to repair the *Hercules* in an English harbour'. *Brazen* was the name, and brazen was the deed; once clear of Barbados, the *Hercules* was boarded for the second time and escorted to Antigua. Here, 'The ship and property was proceeded against for a breach of some or one of the laws of trade and navigation, condemned and sold by public auction at great sacrifice. When taking the specie, etc., from on board the *Hercules* before condemnation there was not even a two real piece left me, nor yet a silver spoon.'

Brown took passage to England, arriving in London in June 1817 to contest the sentence; but was informed by the Lords Commissioners of the Treasury that the appeal must be made to the Vice Admiralty Court at Antigua. Early in 1818 the Admiralty Court reversed its earlier decision, but ruled that the proceeds of the auction must be shared with the agents of the King of Spain. Brown's troubles were not yet at an end, because the Government of La Plata had also laid claim to the property, and on his return to Buenos Aires he was promptly arrested. 'The unfortunate exit of the expedition had caused impressions in the minds of the inhabitants very unfavourable indeed towards my person and character. I was confined in a military prison the third day after landing for forty days and afterwards tried by a military Court Martial that lasted nearly a year . . .'

He was eventually exonerated and retained his rank of Admiral, but his spirits were now at low ebb, especially because there had been a change of regime in his absence and the new Supreme Director, Puyrredón, had indicated that his wife and family were no longer welcome and insisted on their return to England. 'This [the court martial] and the injustice which I met with in England bore hard on my mind, separated too from my family which perhaps eer long might be in need of the necessities of life and perhaps in want of bread. I caught a typhus fever about the middle of Sept. 1819 which on the 23rd having deprived me of my senses I threw myself off the top of Mr. Reid's house three story high broke my thigh bone and comitted other acts which I hope the Almighty will forgive. After this accident I laid six months on the broad on my back without being able to move a limb or my body and God but knows what I suffered.'

Brown's services to the Provinces of the Río de la Plata were by no means over and he was later to obtain honourable amends for his shabby treatment. Until he resumed active command of the navy in 1825 in the offensive against Brazil (see Chapter VIII), he devoted himself to his trading interests. In the meantime the liberation of Chile and Peru, in whose cause he had fired some of the first defiant shots, was to be achieved with the energetic participation of a band of equally daring British adventurers.

III SEAMAN EXTRAORDINARY

O F all the provinces of Spain's American empire, the richest and most influential was the viceroyalty of Peru. Pizarro had designated its capital, Lima, as 'The City of Kings'; and it remained the focus of the entrenched power of *peninsulares* from the mother country. After the *porteños* of Buenos Aires had set up their Provisional Junta in 1810 and embarked on the course which was to lead to complete independence, it was therefore natural that they should regard Peru as the main antagonist.

Worsted in a direct attack through Upper Peru, the Buenos Aires Junta turned its attention to the neighbouring and much poorer captain-generalship of Chile, where the creoles greatly outnumbered native-born Spaniards. As early as the summer of 1810 a *porteño* envoy, Álvarez de Jonte, was preaching revolution in Santiago; and in September the Spanish Captain-General was deposed and a Junta of seven leading citizens assumed power. Although in the first place the Junta ruled nominally on behalf of the exiled Ferdinand VII, it was hardly to be expected that the Authorities in Peru, of which Chile had always been a dependency, would allow this rebuff to go unchallenged. An Irish soldier, General MacKenna, played a leading part during the first phase of hostilities.

John MacKenna left his native Ireland at the age of eleven to study at the Royal Engineering Academy in Barcelona, and after seeing service with the Spanish army in Morocco and against the French in the war of 1794, embarked for Peru in 1796. The Viceroy in Lima at the time was his compatriot Ambrosio O'Higgins, who, from starting life as the son of a peasant farmer and page to the Dowager Countess of Bective, had become the most important officer of the Spanish Crown in South America – this as a result of his splendid record in building roads, promoting agriculture and in winning over the Indians by his conciliatory policies. O'Higgins was warm in his welcome and made use of MacKenna's talents as an engineer to construct roads and bridges and also to renew the fortifications of the great Spanish base of Valdivia in the south of Chile – ironically enough to be demolished a few years later by Admiral Cochrane and Major Miller, fighting for the patriots in the footsteps of MacKenna himself.

It seems that MacKenna changed sides as the result of his marriage to Josefa Vicuña Marrain, a girl of good Chilean family with creole sympathies. At any rate, when the Spanish Captain-General was deposed, he was asked to prepare plans for the defence of the country, was appointed Governor of Valparaiso in January 1811 and became a member of the Junta with the rank of Commander-General of Artillery.

During a first and unsuccessful attempt of the royalists to regain power, in Spring 1811, the three forceful but unprincipled Carrera brothers seized the opportunity to topple the patriot government and to set up a new Junta in their own interests. MacKenna was removed from his command and subsequently banished to his farm in the country, from which he was recalled when, early in 1813, the Peruvian Viceroy, Abascal, despatched an army, which landed in southern Chile and seized the city of Concepción.

Command of the patriot army now passed to Bernardo O'Higgins, the English-educated son of the famous Viceroy, who, with José de San Martín, shares the credit for the final liberation of the country. During 1813–14 O'Higgins and MacKenna scored various successes against the Spaniards, notably at Membrillar, near Concepción, where MacKenna, much outnumbered by the royalists, won a brilliant victory. However, O'Higgins, left in the lurch by the unreliable Carreras, was badly defeated by the Spaniards at Rancagua in 1814, and both they, O'Higgins and MacKenna made their escape across the Andes to the United Provinces of La Plata and their capital, Buenos Aires.

The feud between MacKenna and the Carreras flared up once again, and when Luis Carrera, the youngest of the brothers, arrived in Buenos Aires, it was to find that they were lodged in the same street. What next ensued is graphically described by Mulhall: 'Carrera sent MacKenna a challenge for some alleged comments upon his brother. A duel came off at mid-night (Nov. 21st 1814) at Videla's quinta, near Barracas, Admiral Brown being Carrera's second, and Col. Vargas MacKenna's. At the first interchange of shots, MacKenna's bullet went through his adversary's hat; at the second MacKenna fell dead, having received a ball in the throat. The corpse was conveyed to Sto. Domingo church next morning and buried there.' Luis Carrera did not long survive the duel, meeting his death at the hands of a firing squad at Santiago in 1818 – the supposition being that General San Martín, who ordered the execution, was in no mind to risk a challenge to his authority or to brook their further intrigues.

THE NEW CONQUISTADORS

With the flight of O'Higgins and the Carreras in the autumn of 1814, Chile reverted to Spanish rule. Confiscation, prosecution and imprisonment were the order of the day; but, over the border, at Mendoza in the shadow of the Andes, José de San Martín was preparing for the final liberation of the country. Born in the United Provinces, he had trained with the army in Spain, and on offering his services to the Buenos Aires Junta he was ordered to mount a fresh attack through Upper Peru. However, he became convinced that the viceroyalty could be toppled only by an indirect assault through Chile, and from 1814 to 1817, with the support of O'Higgins, he built up the 5000-strong Army of the Andes with recruits from Chile, patriots from the Provinces of the Rio de la Plata and foreign soldiers of fortune.

Before the army began its historic passage of the Andes in January 1817, it was another Irish soldier, John Thomond O'Brien, San Martín's aide-de-camp and, in Mulhall's words, 'An impressive figure, standing nearly 6½ feet in height', who went ahead with a picked force of three hundred men to clear the snow. It was a task that proved so rigorous that it cost him half his men; and the perils of the advance into Chile over mountains standing more than two miles above sea-level can be judged by an extract from San Martín's own account:

> The army had 10,600 saddle and pack mules, 1500 horses, and 700 head of cattle, and despite the most scrupulous care there arrived in Chile only 4,300 mules and 511 horses in very bad condition . . . Food supplies for the twenty days the march was to last were taken on mule-back, inasmuch as there was no house or town between Mendoza and Chile . . . and five mountain ranges had to be crossed. The greater part of the army suffered from lack of oxygen, as a result of which several soldiers died, besides others who succumbed to the intense cold . . .

Emerging from the mountains, the Army of the Andes surprised a royalist force of 4,000 at Chacabuco on the road to Santiago. The first attack by O'Higgins's infantry brigade was repulsed with severe loss; San Martín then launched his cavalry, and the Spaniards broke and fled, leaving 600 dead on the field. O'Brien, who had distinguished himself by galloping up to the enemy lines and capturing the royal standard, was later sent in pursuit of the fugitives towards Valparaiso. Amongst their baggage he laid hands on the military chest, consisting of 1700 doubloons (about £6000) in two saddle bags, which he forwarded to San Martín. It is an ironical comment on mercenary morals that he was publicly thanked by the government for his honesty in surrendering the money.

O'Brien was to serve San Martín loyally throughout his campaigns, and Mulhall recounts that 'On the day (July 28th 1821) when Independence was declared at Lima the Protector harangued his army in the great plaza, and taking in his hand the standard of Pizarro he said "this is my portion of the trophies." Then taking the state canopy of Pizarro, a kind of umbrella always borne over the Viceroys in processions, he presented it to Gen. O'Brien, saying "This is for the gallant comrade who has fought so many years by my side in the cause of South-America." This canopy is now in the possession of Gen. O'Brien's daughter; it is 24 feet circumference, of rich crimson velvet embroidered with gold, and has attached to it the following note in O'Brien's writing "This canopy was brought to Peru on Pizarro's second journey from Spain. It was held over him and all subsequent Vice-Kings of Peru on state occasions. Little did they think its last owner would be an Irishman!" '

Now and later, the army stood in need of medical services; and it was the English-born Dr James Paroissien who directed them. Of Huguenot extraction, he had arrived in Montevideo at the age of twenty-two in 1807 and after its evacuation by Sir Samuel Auchmuty had been forced to depart for Rio de Janeiro. A young man of varied talents besides medicine, he happened to hear that the Prince Regent of Portugal needed butter, then unobtainable in Brazil, and for a time managed his dairy. He was next involved in the intrigues of the Princess Carlota Joaquina and Sir Sidney Smith (see page 31) and was arrested in Buenos Aires as a secret agent. Released during the revolution, he accompanied the *porteño* army on its disastrous expedition to Upper Peru in 1810 as a surgeon and later became director of a gunpowder factory in the northern city of Córdoba – an appointment which came to an abrupt end when the factory blew up. In September 1816 he was gazetted chief surgeon to the Army of the Andes and was commended by San Martín for his 'humanity and devotion' to the wounded. He later served as one of the General's chief aides-de-camp during the campaign in Peru and was one of two delegates entrusted with raising a loan for the Peruvian government in London. On San Martín's retirement, Paroissien became involved in a speculative scheme for exploiting silver mines in Potosí and died a ruined man while on his return voyage to England.

William Miller, whose selfless devotion to the patriot cause won the respect of insurgents and Spaniards alike, arrived in Chile in 1818 on the eve of the Battle of Maipú, which confirmed the country's independence. A native of Kent, he joined the British army at sixteen and both served with Wellington in the Peninsula and took part in the abortive attack on New Orleans in 1814, the final engagement in a war with the United States, precipitated by the British blockade of French ports, and the last occasion on which British and American soldiers met as enemies. On his return to England, like many other Peninsular veterans, 'he soon grew tired of inactivity; and turning his attention to the state of the struggle between Spanish America and the mother country, considered, after due inquiry, that the River Plate was the most eligible point to which he could direct his course. Few English candidates for military fame had proceeded to that country; and this was the reason why Mr. Miller preferred it to Columbia, already overrun with adventurers of all descriptions.'

He arrived in Buenos Aires in September 1817, where it seems that 'some tempting prospects and advantages of a lucrative nature were placed before his view', and first made an extensive trip on horseback across the *pampas* to the south. In an interesting ecological note he comments on the wanton slaughter of cattle for their hides, remarking that 'The flesh, which would have sufficed to feed a numerous army in Europe, was left on the plain to be devoured by tigers, wild dogs, and ravens.'

However, his original resolve to join the Army of the Andes was reinforced 'by the opinion of an English lady, who, after some preliminary conversation, observed, "I find that there exists a wish to prevail upon you to devote yourself to money-making pursuits. Now, I dissent from this well-intentioned advice. Were I a young man, I would never abandon the career of glory for the sake of gain." In eight and forty hours from the time of that conversation [on 6 January, 1818], Miller took an affectionate leave of the lady, of her husband (Mr. M'Kinlay), and of their numerous family, from all of whom he had received the kindest attention during his stay in Buenos Ayres.'

Miller rode the 600 miles in nine days and, crossing the Andes by the route which had taken San Martín's army three weeks, reached Santiago three and a half days later. On proceeding to San Martín's headquarters, he was assigned to the Buenos Airean artillery. Used as he was to the pipeclay and polish of the British army, he was at first taken aback by the appearance of the troops. 'A man on guard without a stock, and perhaps without a button to his coat, was a strange sight to one accustomed to see well-dressed soldiers. Yet the composition of the army of the Andes was good, and although the dress of the soldiers was unsightly, they were well armed, tolerably disciplined, and enthusiastic. National airs and hymns to liberty, accompanied by the sound of guitars, were heard throughout the encampment every evening till a late hour.'

After the patriots' reverse at Cancharayda in March 1818 and shortly before their decisive victory at Maipú, Miller was seconded to the frigate *Lautaro* in command of a company of marines, The ship, an old East-Indiaman of 800 tons, had been hastily purchased in case it proved necessary to evacuate the government; and Miller had this to say about her crew: 'She was officered principally by Englishmen. Her ship's company was composed of one hundred foreign seamen, two hundred and fifty Chilenos, most of whom had never been afloat, besides the above-mentioned marines. The Chilenos were so eager to go upon the service, that several swam off to the frigate. As soon as the motley but enthusiastic crew was hurried on board, the ship got under weigh in a state ill calculated for immediate action. The Europeans had just before received bounty money, and, of all the ship's company, were the least efficient from inebriety, whilst hardly a naval officer could give an order in the Spanish language . . .'

In spite of these disadvantages, the *Lautaro* had the better of a brush with the Spanish warships *Esmeralda* and *Pezuela*; and O'Higgins, who had now become Supreme Director (San Martín having declined the office), energetically set about the creation of a Chilean navy. When the squadron of four ships, the *San Martín*, *Lautaro*, *Chacabuco* and *Araucano*, for whose purchase the well-to-do of Santiago had sacrificed plate and possessions, put to sea in October 1818, Miller was again in command of the marines. 'Foreigners, who were candidates for the [naval] command, were so exorbitant on their conditions, and so divided amongst themselves' that O'Higgins eventually appointed a young Chilean, Manuel Blanco Encalada, with instructions to intercept a large Spanish convoy, en route from Cadiz with reinforcements. The operation proved to be an unqualified success, the Spanish flagship, the *Reina María Isabel*, being captured and the transports with their 2800 troops seized or dispersed. It nevertheless came near to being Miller's last.

After an exchange of salvos with the *San Martín*, the *María Isabel* had been driven ashore; part of her crew struggled on to the beach; and Miller was despatched with a flag of truce to offer terms. On landing, he was immediately surrounded and threatened at musketpoint. Two militia officers now appeared and walked him two miles inland to meet General Sanchez, the Spanish commander.

By Miller's own account, 'General Sánchez passed on without deigning to speak to Major Miller, but ordered him to be blind-folded. The militia officers, encouraged by this appearance of harshness, increased their former incivility, and became brutally insulting. One of them poured forth an uninterrupted torrent of abuse for nearly two hours, and then desired two men to tighten the handkerchief over the major's eyes, which they did with all their strength. Sanchez at length ordered the prisoner to be brought into his presence, to communicate the commodore's proposals. The general listened to them with the utmost contempt, and, with a roughness of manner which showed that he was a stranger to the commonest forms of good breeding, gave for an answer that the bearer should be *despatched* in the way he deserved.'

Fortunately, he was befriended by two senior officers, one of whom discovered that, during his service in the Peninsula, Miller had made close friends with some of his own fellow officers. They accordingly spoke up on his behalf. 'At first Sánchez refused to listen to them, and it was not until the colonels had given some intelligible hints, comparing the number and quantity of the bayonets in their respective battalions with the other forces of the general, that he reluctantly gave way . . .' Miller was then led back to the beach and allowed to remove the bandage. 'All thought that he had fallen a sacrifice, and his unexpected return was greeted with hearty cheers. He found that his marines and *cholos* [Chilean recruits], upon hearing of his detention, went aft in a body, and requested the commodore to permit them to land and rescue their commandant.'

Blanco Encalada was twenty-eight and prior to his victory in Talcahuano Bay on 28 October, 1818, had seen service only as a midshipman in the Spanish navy. He spoke nothing but his native Spanish, so that Miller could write of a subsequent emergency when the *San Martín* struck a sandbank: 'The confusion was inde-scribable. The only naval officer on board, excepting the commo-dore, was the first lieutenant, who, on the day before, had become deaf from the effects of firing, and now became dumb, or at least so hoarse as to be unable to make himself heard; and the commodore, being ignorant of the English language, could not himself give orders to the foreign seamen. Major Miller, the surgeon, and the purser, were therefore the only three officers capable of com-municating an order; but as none of them understood any thing of seamanship, the scene became truly distressing.'

It was for reasons such as these that rather more than a year before, in the spring of 1817, O'Higgins had despatched an envoy to London, José Álvarez Condarco, to engage a commander for the embryo Chilean navy. In the person of a Scottish nobleman who was a strange amalgam of a superb naval tactician, a sailor of unsurpassed courage and an aristocrat, at once authoritarian yet outspokenly radical in his political views, Álvarez found a man uniquely suited for the task in hand. It was under Lord Cochrane that Miller was to come into his own in a series of brilliant amphibious operations along the shores of Chile and Peru.

'The Cochranes,' it has been said in Scotland, 'have long been noted for an original and dashing turn of mind, which was sometimes called genius, sometimes eccentricity.' Of none of the family is this more true than of Thomas, the Tenth Earl of Dundonald, who was born at Annsfield in Lanarkshire in 1775. His father was a scientific amateur; but unlike his contemporaries, Cavendish, Black, Priestly and Watt, who, as Cochrane writes in his *Autobiography of a Seaman*, 'prudently confined their attentions to their laboratories, my father's sanguine expectations of retrieving the family estates by his discoveries led him to embark in a multitude of manufacturing projects'.

Unfortunately the Ninth Earl was a better inventor than business man; the family fortune melted 'like the flux in his crucibles'; and, as Cochrane continues, 'Unsuccessful everywhere, my father turned his attention to myself'. Thomas was destined for a career in the army, but decided that he wanted to go to sea. Thanks to the good offices of his uncle, Sir Alexander (later Admiral) Cochrane, he joined the navy at the age of seventeen. 'The difficulty was to equip me for sea, but it was obviated by the Earl of Hopetoun considerately advancing 100*l* for the purpose. With this sum the requisite outfit was procured, and a few days placed me in a position to seek my fortune, with my father's gold watch as a keepsake – the only patrimony I ever inherited.'

To these early experiences may be attributed Cochrane's abiding interest in scientific novelties, such as Congreve rockets and steamships, and also his determination to exact a high price for his services. It was not long before the young man was repairing his fortunes by a series of unconventional attacks on French and Spanish shipping in the Mediterranean. During his first thirteen months of independent command, his little 158-ton brig, the *Speedy*, by daring or by ruses, which included the hoisting of foreign colours or the yellow flag of plague, captured some fifty craft, numbering gun boats, privateers and merchantmen of every size and shape. But it was after Britain's entry into the Peninsular War on the side of Spain in 1808, and in command of the frigate *Impérieuse*, that Cochrane made his name as a naval tactician and perfected the skills which he later employed to such effect in South America.

His most spectacular feat in the Mediterranean, the defence of the Spanish port of Rosas in 1808 against an entire French army, has been graphically described in *Peter Simple* by Captain Marryat, who first served in the navy as a midshipman in the *Impérieuse*. Equally daring was his attack in April 1809 on fourteen capital ships of the French Atlantic fleet, lying in the security of the Basque Roads in the English Channel. With no more than a single frigate and a few fire-ships he successfully blew up the harbour boom and, as Napoleon wrote later, 'would have destroyed or taken all the French ships at Aix, if, as was his due, he had been supported by the English admiral [Lord Gambier]'.

Cochrane was never backward in denouncing cowardice or incompetence – even that of his superiors – and it was criticism of Gambier, leading to the Admiral's being tried before a court martial, that brought to the boil a long-standing feud with the Admiralty. It had begun with his addressing a series of high-handed letters to the First Lord of Admiralty, Lord St. Vincent, over delays in promotion and abuses in the distribution of prize money. After being elected to Parliament, first as radical member for Honiton in 1806, and subsequently for Westminster, he broadened the attack with repeated denunciations of the rampant profiteering in the dockyards and the disgraceful lot of the common sailor. As far as St. Vincent was concerned, the onslaught was misdirected, since he was as much opposed to fraudulent contractors as was Cochrane himself. Intemperate and personal attacks brought stinging rejoinders: thus St. Vincent wrote of the Cochranes that 'they are all mad, romantic, money-getting, and not truth-telling', whilst one of Cochrane's commanders in the Mediterranean, Lord Keith, was sorry to find him 'wrong-headed, violent and proud'.

In a Tory parliament whose leading parties he had contemptuously dubbed the 'ins' and the 'outs', he had few supporters apart from his fellow radicals, William Cobbet and Sir Francis Burdett; and a speech like that in which he equated the Wellesleys' emoluments of £34,729 from the public funds to 425 pairs of lieutenant's legs (calculated at the rate of a pension awarded to a maimed naval officer) only infuriated the Tory establishment. In his own words, he became a 'marked man'; and his fall was as spectacular as his rise.

Bernardo O'Higgins, Supreme Director of Chile.

José de San Martín.

San Martín's army crossing the Andes.

Left William Miller.

Right Lord Cochrane at the time of the Stock Exchange trial.

Far right Lord Cochrane as a young man.

Below The Battle of Chacabuco.

Right The bombardment of Callao by Lord Cochrane.

Left A Tucumano with his *laso* and a Peruvian soldier on the march.

Above Lord Cochrane's house at Quintero and *(right)* a Peruvian cavalryman. *Below* The Bay of Quintero.

Late on the night of Sunday, 20 February, 1814, a young man knocked at the Ship Inn at Dover and, throwing off a scarlet uniform, announced himself as a Colonel du Bourg with important news for the Port Admiral. His 'news' was of the defeat of Napoleon; and it soon spread to the London Stock Exchange, where it caused an immediate furore and a sharp rise in securities, among them one in which Cochrane had invested £139,000, the proceeds of prize money. When it turned out that du Bourg was an impostor and an acquaintance of Cochrane – who, of course, stood to gain by the fraud – a High Court writ was issued. Cochrane, with his business associates, was found guilty and savagely sentenced to a £1000 fine, a year's imprisonment and to standing in the stocks at the Royal Exchange. Since the Lord Chief Justice, Lord Ellenborough, was of the Tory elite and the evidence far from conclusive, the verdict has been argued ever since. However, the authorities, acting with indecent haste, stripped Cochrane of his honours, Bath King of Arms causing his banner to be kicked down the steps of Westminster Abbey and the Admiralty removing his name from the Navy List. If he was spared the ultimate indignity of standing in the pillory, it was because Lord Castlereagh feared that the appearance of a popular hero would incite a riot and hastily abolished the practice.

Cochrane emerged from prison with his career in ruins; but, if not by the government at home, his talents as a seaman extraordinary were recognized abroad – not least by the exiled Napoleon (the respect was mutual, since at one point Cochrane seriously entertained a scheme for rescuing Napoleon from St. Helena and installing him as Emperor of South America). It was, ironically enough, shortly after turning down a similar offer from Spain that he was approached by the Chilean envoy; and Álvarez was justifiably elated when he wrote to the Supreme Director that 'I have extreme satisfaction in informing you that Lord Cochrane, one of the most eminent and valiant seamen of Great Britain, has undertaken to proceed to Chile to direct our navy. He is a person highly commendable, not only on account of the liberal principles with which he has always upheld the English people in their Parliament, but also because he bears a character altogether superior to ambitious self-seeking.'

Together with his wife and two young children, Cochrane arrived in Valparaiso on 28 November, 1818, hard on the heels of Blanco Encalada's squadron, fresh from its victory over the Spaniards, and was fêted in a succession of balls and receptions, including an open air performance of *Othello*. 'The two presiding *belles*,' as Miller reports, 'were Lady Cochrane and Mrs. Commodore Blanco, both young, fascinating, and highly gifted.' (Cochrane, though professing that he was 'without a particle of romance in his composition', had in fact first seen his future wife at the age of sixteen in a school crocodile in Hyde Park and promptly eloped with her.) It was not long before he felt that these junketings were 'being prolonged for so many days as to be a waste of time'; and in fact there seems to have been more behind them than meets the eye.

O'Higgins had not bargained for the spectacular success of the youthful Blanco Encalada; and there were those among his ministers who now argued that 'it was dangerous and discreditable to a republican government to allow a nobleman and a foreigner to command its navy . . . the object being to place Admiral Blanco in the chief command . . .' More seriously, 'It so happened that two of the Chilean commanders, Captains Guise and Spry, had shortly before arrived from England with the *Hecate*, which had been sold out of the British navy and bought by them on speculation . . . These officers, together with Captain Worcester, a North American, got up a cabal, the object of which was to bring about a divided command between myself and Admiral Blanco, or, as they expressed it – "two commodores and no Cochrane."' Fortunately, Blanco Encalada refused to be drawn into the intrigue; O'Higgins, who has been described as having 'too much wax and too little steel in his composition', nevertheless stuck to his bargain; and on 22 December, 1818, Cochrane was formally appointed 'Vice-Admiral of Chile, Admiral and Commander-in-Chief of the Naval Forces of the Republic'.

His fleet, which had strained the resources of the young republic to breaking point, comprised:

> *San Martín* 1300 tons and 56 guns
> *O'Higgins* (the renamed *María Isabel*), 1200 tons and 50 guns
> *Lautaro* 850 tons and 48 guns
> *Chacabuco* 450 tons and 20 guns
> *Galvarino* (the renamed *Hecate*), 398 tons and 18 guns
> *Araucano* 270 tons and 16 guns
> *Puyrredón* 220 tons and 16 guns

Cochrane had brought with him from England a nucleus of reliable officers; Miller, as his commander of marines, was a tower of strength; but the equipment and manning of the ships was to prove a major problem. Of the 2200 men he recruited during the next month, the bulk were *cholos* (or untried Chilean peasants); and these were stiffened with an extraordinary mixture of foreign mercenaries – British, North American and Chinese. Both Cochrane and the government were impatient for action, and by devoting his formidable energies to getting ready four of the ships for sea, he was able to steer north for Peru on 16 January with his flagship, the *O'Higgins*, the *San Martín*, *Lautaro* and *Chacabuco*, leaving Admiral Blanco to follow with the others.

As the flotilla was about to put to sea, Lady Cochrane was horrified to see her five-year-old son, Thomas, run down the beach, waving his hat and shouting *'Viva la patria'*; and powerless to intervene, watched as he was put into a boat by her husband's flag-lieutenant and ferried out to the *O'Higgins*, now underway. A few weeks later the small boy was to have his first taste of action, as Cochrane relates in his *Narrative of Services in the Liberation of Chili, Peru, and Brazil*: 'When the firing commenced, I had placed the boy in my after-cabin, locking the door upon him; but not liking the restriction, he contrived to get through the quarter gallery window, and joined me on deck, refusing to go down again. As I could not attend to him, he was permitted to remain, and, in a miniature midshipman's uniform, which the seamen had made for him, was busying himself in handing powder to the gunners.

'Whilst thus employed, a round shot took off the head of a marine close to him, scattering the unlucky man's brains in his face. Instantly recovering his self-possession, to my great relief, for believing him killed, I was spell-bound with agony, he ran up to me exclaiming, "I am not hurt, papa: the shot did not touch me; Jack says, the ball is not made that can kill mamma's boy." I ordered him to be carried below; but, resisting with all his might, he was permitted to remain on deck during the action.'

Cochrane's objective was the port of Callao, six miles from Lima and some 1500 north of Valparaiso, and the most important of Spain's naval bases in the Pacific. When he arrived with his small squadron on 21 February, 1819, it was to find that there were two frigates, the *Esmeralda* and *Venganza*, a corvette, three brigs of war, twenty-eight gunboats and six heavily-armed merchantmen in the harbour, moored under shore batteries mounting 160 guns. Since a direct attack was out of the question, Cochrane decided to repeat the tactics which had proved so successful when, heavily outgunned and in the face of overwhelming odds, he had seized the frigate *El Gamo* in his onslaught on the French and their Spanish allies during the run-up to the Peninsular War.

THE NEW CONQUISTADORS

The Mardi Gras festival was at its height, and two North American warships were expected at Callao on a visit. His plan was to sail boldly into the bay under American colours, to stage a diversion by sending a boat ashore with despatches and simultaneously to dash in and cut out the Spanish frigates. At this point a thick fog came down; and hearing the sound of heavy firing, Cochrane imagined that his other ships were already engaged and stood into the harbour – only to discover that the firing was a salute to the Viceroy from a Spanish gunboat, which he promptly seized. Alert to the danger, the Viceroy now warned the shore batteries, and when the Chilean squadron attempted to press home the attack, it was driven back by salvos from the forts, as a result of which Captain Guise, in command of the *Lautaro*, was severely wounded. The Spaniards were nevertheless so rattled that they dismantled the top masts and spars of their warships so as to make a boom across the anchorage. Although the outcome was not all that Cochrane had planned, it earned him the 'not very complimentary' nickname of *El Diablo* and, by confining the Spanish navy to port, ensured the lifting of its blockade of Valparaiso.

His next step was to seize the off-shore island of San Lorenzo as a base for further operations and to release a number of Chilean captives kept there in chains. When he further suggested an exchange of Spanish and Chilean prisoners, the Viceroy, Pezuela, peremptorily turned down the offer, expressing his surprise that 'a British nobleman should command the maritime forces of a Government "unacknowledged by all the Powers of the globe"'. To this, Cochrane at once retorted that 'a British nobleman was a free man, and therefore had a right to adopt any country which was endeavouring to re-establish the rights of aggrieved humanity; and that I had hence adopted the cause of Chili, with the same freedom of judgment that I had previously exercised when refusing the offer of an Admiral's rank in Spain, made to me not long before, by the Spanish Ambassador in London.'

Cochrane now decided to launch an attack with fire-ships, and in the words of Miller's *Memoirs*, 'A laboratory was formed upon San Lorenzo, under the superintendence of Major Miller. On the 19th of March, an accidental explosion took place, which scorched the major and ten men in a dreadful manner. The former lost the nails from both hands, and the injury was so severe that his face was swelled to twice its natural dimensions . . . He was blind and delirious for some days, and was confined to his cabin for six weeks.' The sequel was equally unfortunate, since, when the fire-ship was towed in on the 22nd, she came under heavy fire from the forts and 'grounded within a musket shot of them, knocked a hole in her bottom, and filled'.

After a cruise northwards along the Peruvian coast to reconnoitre and to revictual his ships – 'it being my practice to compel the Spaniards to supply all the wants of the squadron, nothing being ever taken from the natives without payment' – Cochrane dropped anchor at Valparaiso on 16 June and began preparations for a further attack on Callao.

Among the English contingent who had sailed with him to Chile was a Mr Goldsack, an assistant of Sir William Congreve, the inventor of the rockets which Cochrane had used to such good effect during his attack on the Basque Roads. Goldsack was now set to work to manufacture rockets in quantity; but, as Cochrane relates, 'From a mistaken notion of parsimony, the labour of constructing and filling them was allotted to a number of Spanish prisoners, with what results will appear in the sequel'. By 29 September the squadron was again off Callao. The attack, of which so much was expected, took place a few days later; and in the words of Miller, who led it:

'Not more than one rocket in six went off properly. Some burst, from the badness of the cylinders; some took a wrong direction, in consequence of the sticks being made of knotty wood; and most of them fell short. The shells sunk a gun-boat, and did some execution in the forts and amongst the shipping; but the lashings of the mortar-bed gave way, and it was with difficulty that the logs of which the raft was composed were kept together. A great deal of time was lost in repairing the defective state of the fastenings. Day-light began to appear, and the rockets having completely failed, the rafts were ordered to retire, and were towed off . . .'

Some twenty sailors and marines were killed or wounded during the abortive attack, one of them, Lieutenant Bayley, 'a very brave young man and a most active officer', being cut in two by a round shot, while others were badly burned by the premature explosion of the rockets. Cochrane adds his own chagrined footnote, explaining that the 'Spanish prisoners . . . as was found on examination, had embraced every opportunity of inserting handfulls of sand, sawdust, and even manure, at intervals in the tubes, thus impeding the process of combustion, whilst in the majority of instances they had so thoroughly mixed the neutralizing matter with the ingredients supplied, that the charge would not ignite at all, the result being complete failure in the object of the expedition . . .'

Cochrane was acutely discomforted by the débâcle, as he was by this time at cross purposes with the Chilean Minister of Marine, Zenteno, whom he blamed for lack of support in the operation: 'My instructions, as has been said, were carefully drawn up to prevent my doing anything rash – as the first trip to Callao had been represented by certain officers under my command, who had no great relish for fighting.' At the same time he was aware that 'the Chilean people expected impossibilities', and the success of a raid on Pisco, further south – during which the commander of the patriot infantry, Colonel Charles, was killed and Miller so severely wounded as to hover between life and death for seventeen days – was not in itself enough. Before returning to Valparaiso, Cochrane was determined to have something more solid to his credit. It was thus that he conceived the idea of an attack on Valdivia, far south of Valparaiso, approximately one third of the distance to Cape Horn, and a Spanish base so formidable that it was known as the Gibraltar of South America.

The feud with Captains Guise and Spry had reopened, when they accused Cochrane of appropriating more than his fair share of prize money and he in turn taxed them with fomenting a mutiny. It was therefore with a single vessel, the flagship *O'Higgins*, that he beat to the south. In his own words: 'The enterprise was a desperate one; nevertheless, I was not about to do anything desperate, having resolved that, unless fully satisfied as to its practicality, I would not attempt it. Rashness, though often imputed to me, forms no part of my composition. There is rashness without calculation of consequences; but with that calculation, well-founded, it is no longer rashness. And thus, now that I was unfettered by people who did not second my operations as they ought to have done, I made up my mind to take Valdivia, if the attempt came within the scope of my calculations.'

On 18 January, when Major Miller appeared on deck for the first time since being wounded at Pisco eleven weeks before, Cochrane hoisted Spanish colours and sailed into the anchorage to reconnoitre. Beyond the narrow entrance, the inlet opens out into a wide bay with three arms, at the bottom of one of which, fourteen miles down the Valdivia river, is the town itself. Miller describes it as 'a capacious basin, bordered by a lofty and impenetrable forest advancing to the water's edge. It is encircled by a chain of forts, which are so placed as not only to defend the entrance, but to enfilade every part of the harbour.'

By good fortune the Spaniards were expecting the frigate *Prueba* –

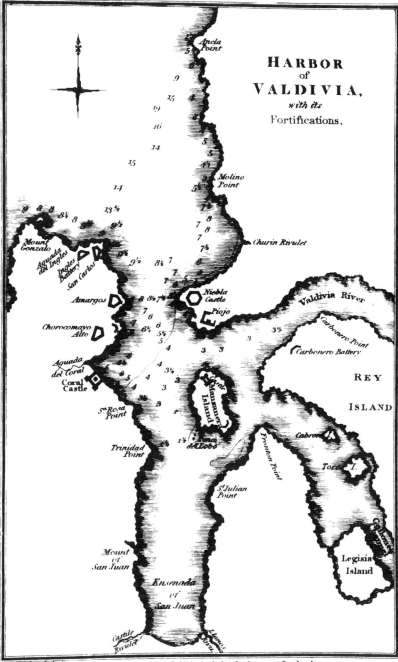

HARBOR
of
VALDIVIA,
with its
Fortifications.

Ancla Point

Molino Point

Churin Rivulet

Mount Gonzalo

Aguada del Ingles

Ingles Battery

San Carlos

Amargos

Chorocomayo Alto

Niebla Castle

Piojo

Valdivia River

Carbonero Point

Carbonero Battery

Aguada del Coral

Coral Castle

Sª Rosa Point

Corral Manzanera Island

REY ISLAND

Cabron

Trinidad Point

Piedra del Lobo

Fronton Point

Cabron

Torr I.

Sᵗ Julian Point

Mount of San Juan

Ensenada of San Juan

Legisia Island

Castle Rivulet

Llanos

Russell & Jons, sculpsit

Published May 15, 1826, by Baldwin, Cradock, & Joy, Paternoster Row, London.

55

which Cochrane had long since bottled up at Guayaquil, far to the north, after his first attack on Callao – and when he boldly signalled for a pilot, they obliged by sending out a boat, whose crew were immediately made prisoner and not only supplied invaluable information about the channels, but divulged that the brig *Potrillo* was daily expected with twenty thousand dollars on board for payment of the garrison. The ship was duly captured after a three hour chase; and Cochrane then made for Concepción further to the north to ask for reinforcements from its Governor, General Freire. Freire, like Cochrane, had his differences with the government – he was later, indeed, to overturn O'Higgins – and the fact that the expedition was unauthorized by the Chilean authorities did not prevent his making available 250 men, who were duly embarked in the *O'Higgins*, the schooner *Montezuma* and a brig of war from Buenos Aires, the *Intrépido*, which volunteered for the attempt.

The little flotilla set course for Valdivia on the evening of 25 January, and Cochrane, short of officers and overcome by fatigue, left the watch to a midshipman, who promptly fell asleep. In the meantime a breeze sprang up, and the *O'Higgins* struck a reef off Quiriquina Island. Having towed her off with kedges, Cochrane at first refused to inspect the damage, remarking to Miller: '"Well, Major, Valdivia we must take. Sooner than put back, it would be better if we all went to the bottom . . ."'

It was only at sunset on the 26th, with the ships still forty miles offshore, that it was discovered that there were five feet of water in the hold and that the pumps were out of order. At this juncture Cochrane took off his jacket and with his own hands succeeded in getting two of the pumps into working order. The powder magazine had been flooded, and the marines were left only with the cartridges in their bandoliers; but Cochrane had no doubts about pressing on, reckoning that cold steel would be as effective as powder and shot.

Leaving the crippled *O'Higgins* out of sight offshore, so as to avoid raising Spanish suspicions, Cochrane transferred the troops and marines to the two smaller ships, with which he now stood in and anchored off Fort Inglés, commanding the entrance to the harbour. To a Spanish demand for a boat to be sent ashore for a pilot, he answered through a Spanish volunteer that the ships had become separated from a convoy out of Cadiz during a storm off Cape Horn, in which all their small craft had been lost. Unsatisfied by this reply, the Spanish fired alarm guns and began massing troops below the fort. When one of the two launches being prepared for the attack in the lee of the vessels drifted astern and into sight in the heavy swell, the game was up.

Miller nevertheless pushed off in one of the launches with forty-four marines and made for the shore, impeded by the swell, by an accumulation of seaweed, which 'loaded the oars at every stroke', and by a brisk fire from the beachhead. Once again he came within a hair's breadth of death: 'Amongst others the coxswain was wounded, upon which Major Miller took the helm. He seated himself on a spare oar, but finding the seat inconvenient, he had the oar removed, by which he somewhat lowered his position. He had scarcely done so, when a ball passed through his hat, and grazed the crown of his head.'

Having established a footing, the troops were reinforced by some three hundred more from the ships and shortly after sunset they 'advanced in single files along the rocky track, leading to Fort Inglés, rendered slippery by the spray of the surf, which dashed, with deafening noise, upon the shore. This noise was rather favourable than otherwise to the adventurous party.' The royalist detachment meanwhile fell back, re-entering the fort by a ladder, which they drew up after them over the ramparts.

One side of Fort Inglés overlooked the sea, but another was over-hung by the branches of the surrounding trees. While Miller and the main party occupied the garrison by a noisy frontal assault, a young Chilean officer, Ensign Vidal, crept under the walls to the rear and, taking advantage of the cover, bridged the ramparts with some loosened pallisades and dropped into the interior, where with a handful of men he made short work of the surprised garrison. Some three hundred Spanish reinforcements had meanwhile formed up near the fort, but fled in terror into the trees and along the narrow track towards the forts further inland.

Such was the confusion that no attempt was made to defend them, and when the Chileans arrived at the last, the Castle of Coral, it was to find that the garrison had deserted the guns on the heights above and were taking to boats for Valdivia. Such as remained were rushed and overcome, the fortifications being a bad repair, since part of the rampart had crumbled and filled the surrounding ditch. By daybreak on 4 February, all five forts on the western side of the harbour were in patriot hands; about a hundred Spaniards had been bayonetted during the night and an equal number made prisoner, for the loss, on the Chilean side, of seven dead and nineteen wounded.

The *Intrépido* and *Montezuma* entered the harbour next morning and were embarking troops to storm the positions on the northern side of the bay, when the Spaniards abandoned them, retreating upstream to Valdivia. Towards evening, the waterlogged *O'Higgins* entered port and was run on to a mudflat to keep her afloat during repairs. The *Intrépido*, which had run aground while attempting to cross the harbour, was meanwhile abandoned and subsequently broke up. It was therefore in the little *Montezuma* that Cochrane and Miller, at the head of two hundred troops, pursued the retreating Spaniards along the river to Valdivia. Its Governor, the old and infirm Colonel Montoya, did not await their arrival, but made good his escape to Chiloe Island to the south with his remaining five hundred troops.

So the Spaniards were driven from their last large base on the Chilean mainland. The booty was enormous, and the strategic gains even more significant. John Miller sums them up by saying: 'The acquisition of Valdivia enabled General San Martín to bestow his undivided attention upon the liberation of Peru. It at the same time afforded a great advantage to the patriots, by dispossessing Spain of her best harbour and strongest hold in the Pacific.' Although Miller himself was later, after years of service in South America, military and administrative, to become highly sceptical of 'the famous loans which have turned out to be more prejudicial than useful to Chile and Peru', the fall of Valdivia, by dispelling prospects of the Spaniards' regaining control in Chile, also resulted in the raising of a £1 million in the City of London and its advance to the government.

Cochrane promptly despatched a small vessel to Valparaiso with news of his success, but before himself returning decided to attack Chiloe Island, a staging post for convoys from Spain after their passage of the Straits of Magellan. The odds proved too great, and after a hotly-contested landing the embattled Miller was snatched from his pursuers, 'a grape-shot having passed through the left thigh: the small bones of the right instep were crushed by a four-pounder shot, fired from a gun-boat, and which might have broken the leg but for a rocket, which Major Miller held in his hand, and which changed the direction of the shot'.

With the wounded Miller, Cochrane arrived back in Valparaiso on 27 February, 1820, in the *Montezuma* – as the crippled *O'Higgins* was still undergoing extensive repairs – to find that Captain Guise had returned to Chile rather before the news of the victory at Valdivia and 'had attributed our rocket failure at Callao to my want of skill in their use; the inference desired, being my want of capability to command a squadron'. The ill-disposed Zenteno 'had drawn up an elaborate accusation against me of disobedience to orders, in not having returned, according to my instructions', and such was the bad blood between the two men that the Minister of Marine, far from being placated by the resounding success in the south, declared that 'the conquest of Valdivia "was the act of a madman! that I deserved to have lost my life in the attempt; and even now ought to lose my head for daring to attack such a place *without instructions*, and for exposing the patriot troops to such hazards . . ."'

Complaints such as these were swept aside in a surge of patriotic enthusiasm and by the decision of the Supreme Director, O'Higgins, to strike a medal for presentation to Cochrane and his men, with a citation declaring that 'the capture of Valdivia was the happy result of the devising of an admirably arranged plan, and of the most daring and valorous execution'. The feud between Cochrane and the intimates of General San Martín, notably Zenteno and Bernardo Monteagudo, nevertheless rumbled on and was to prejudice both the preparations and execution of the forthcoming attempt to liberate Peru.

IV TO The CITY OF The KINGS

AFTER the Battle of Maipú in 1818 General San Martín had recrossed the Andes to raise fresh troops. Hardly had he returned to Chile in January 1820, when he was ordered back by the government in Buenos Aires to quell a series of disturbances which had broken out in the Provinces of La Plata. He was not, however, to be diverted from his purpose of liberating Peru. He therefore declined to obey the order, thus causing great offence in Buenos Aires, and felt it his duty to tender his resignation to the officers of the army at large. He was unanimously re-elected to his command.

If the way was now clear for the long-planned invasion of Peru, the breach with La Plata meant that Chile, historically the poor relation, was entirely dependent upon her own strained resources. According to the Spanish Viceroy, Pezuela, there were some twenty-three thousand regulars stationed in Peru at the time, 8500 of them in Lima and Callao and along the Pacific coast, which were to be the first objectives of the Chilean expedition. But the problem was not simply one of logistics: the viceroyalty was the richest in South America, owing its wealth to the mines and plantations, worked by slave labour and controlled by creoles and *peninsulares* with no desire for a Spanish withdrawal. From the outset San Martín therefore addressed himself to a much wider audience – hence his proclamation before sailing:

> Peruvians – Do not think we shall pretend to treat you as a
> conquered people! such a desire could have entered into the
> heads of none but those who are inimical to our common
> happiness. We only aspire to see you free and happy;
> *yourselves will frame your own government*, choosing that
> form which is most consistent with your customs, your
> situations, and your wishes. Consequently, *you will
> constitute a nation as free and independent as ourselves*.

Underlying the antipathy between Cochrane and San Martín, which grew from their first meeting, was the fact that Cochrane saw the expedition in terms of prompt and decisive military action, whereas San Martín was for ever procrastinating, for reasons well-put by his biographer, Bartolomé Mitre: 'The commander-in-chief . . . had two campaigns before him: one military whose plans he carried in his head; the other political . . . The first described a circle, one half of which was drawn along the coast by the keels of Cochrane's ships; the other half through the highlands of Peru by the feet of the flying column under Arenales . . . The second was more complicated. The idea was to foment the moral force of public opinion, stirring up a spirit of insurrection among the Peruvian people . . . From Pisco he flooded the country with proclamations and organized secret agencies in Lima and the interior.'

The first task was to ferry San Martín and his 4000 men to Peru, and in the words of the English mining engineer, John Miers, 'The difficulties attending the equipping and fitting out this expedition were such as can scarcely be conceived by persons unacquainted with the country, and the small resources which existed for such an enterprize. There was no wharf whence stores could be embarked and carried to the ships; there was not even a common crane in the port of Valparaiso, it required all the skill, perseverance, and knowledge of the admiral to convey to his ships the horses, artillery, ammunition, stores, and baggage necessary. It may here also be observed, that this was the first time any Chileno military force, excepting the 250 men taken on board by Lord Cochrane for his attack on Valdivia, had ever been on ship before.'

What added to Cochrane's problems was that the government, no doubt because it was on the verge of bankruptcy, had withheld the back pay of the squadron, so that the men who had stormed Valdivia 'were literally in rags, and destitute of everything'. They had further been refused a penny of prize money on the specious grounds that its capture was a 'restoration', not a conquest. When Cochrane indignantly demanded of Monteagudo 'whether he considered that which had been advanced as just, or according to the law', he met with the reply, 'Certainly not, but I was ordered to write so'.

The Minister of Marine, Zenteno, exacerbated matters by nominating Captain Spry flag captain on board Cochrane's own ship, the *O'Higgins*, at which point the infuriated Cochrane, backed up by five captains (not, of course, including Guise or Spry) and twenty three commissioned officers of the squadron, tendered his formal resignation. Meanwhile, as Cochrane's secretary, William Bennet Stevenson, reports in his *Sixteen Years in Chile and Peru*, the foreign seamen, crucial to the efficient manning of the ships, were so disgusted over the failure to pay their wages that 'although many were unemployed and wandering about the streets of Valparaiso, few would enter themselves at the rendezvous opened for this purpose'.

Faced with the collapse of the expedition, Zenteno climbed down over the appointment of Captain Spry, and San Martín rose to the occasion by clapping Cochrane on the back and declaring: *'Bien, milord, yo soy General del ejercito, y Vd. será Almirante de la esquadra* (Never mind, my lord, I am general of the army, and you shall be Admiral of the squadron).' The government had thoughts of sending out press gangs to recruit the seamen, but both Cochrane and the senior British naval officer in the port, Captain Sherriff, were so much against the proposal that the problem was solved by a proclamation from San Martín, countersigned by Cochrane as guarantor:

> On my entry into Lima, I will punctually pay to all foreign seamen who shall voluntarily enlist into the Chilean service, the whole arrears of their pay, to which, I will also add to each individual, according to his rank, one year's pay over and above his arrears, as premium or reward for his services, if he continue to fulfil his duty to the surrender of that city, and its occupation by the liberating forces.
>
> (Signed) JOSÉ DE SAN MARTÍN
COCHRANE

The departure of the expedition from Valparaiso on 21 August, 1820 is described in Miller's *Memoirs*: 'It was in truth an imposing and exciting spectacle to behold that bay crowded with shipping, under patriot banners, which formerly received only one merchant vessel annually. As the several corps, marching from cantonments, with music playing, through cheering multitudes, severally arrived upon the beach, they were taken off to their respective transports in the greatest order, and without the occurrence of a single accident.

'The population of the capital and of the country had poured into Valparaiso and every avenue was crowded with spectators. Many females who had shared the fortunes of other campaigns were now unavoidably left behind, and their farewell ejaculations, accompanied by the weeping of children, gave deep and distressing interest to the busy scene.'

Cochrane and San Martín at once joined issue on the first objective, Cochrane, typically, being for a lightning attack on Callao and Lima, while San Martín insisted on sounding out the feelings of the inhabitants and progressing in more leisurely and methodical fashion. As a compromise, the fleet first anchored off Pisco, a hundred and fifty miles to the south of Lima, where General Arenales and his detachment were landed for a pincer attack on Lima from the east. Here the squadron remained for the next fifty days, San Martín's object being to recruit slaves from the plantations for his army; but Miller, now promoted to Lieutenant-Colonel, soon found that 'the men under Las Heras having advanced with such extraordinary caution, the owners had time to remove the principal part of their negro property'.

The argument broke out again on 28 September, when the ships arrived off Callao, and San Martín, instead of attacking, ordered Cochrane to disembark the army at Ancón, some twenty miles to the north. The Admiral detached the *San Martín*, *Galvarino* and *Araucano* to escort the transports, but 'The fact was, that – annoyed in common with the whole expedition at this irresolution on the part of General San Martín, I determined that the means of Chile, furnished with great difficulty, should not be wholly wasted, without some attempt at accomplishing the objects of the expedition; and accordingly formed a plan of attack with the three ships which I had kept back – though being apprehensive that my design would be opposed by General San Martín, I had not even mentioned to him my intentions.'

Cochrane's plan, as bold as it was unconventional, was to slip through the harbour boom in small craft under cover of dark and cut out the Spanish flagship, the *Esmeralda*, guarded as she was by twenty-seven gunboats and three hundred shore-based guns, and further 'crowded with the best sailors and marines that could be procured, these sleeping every night at quarters'. The attack took place on the night of 5 November 1820.

Just on midnight the first of the boats, manned by a party of two hundred and forty picked volunteers and led by Cochrane in person, approached the boom. 'The strictest silence, and the exclusive use of cutlasses were enjoined; so that, as the oars were muffled, and the night dark, the enemy had not the least suspicion of the impending attack.' Challenged by a guard-boat, Cochrane threatened the occupants with 'instant death' if they gave the alarm. A few minutes later the boarding parties were storming the *Esmeralda* from both sides.

The Spaniards, taken completely by surprise, rallied and made a stand on the forecastle. Cochrane, who was among the first to board the ship, was knocked back into his boat by a sentry, suffering severe injury from a thole pin which entered his back near the spine. He nevertheless climbed back, only to be shot through the thigh, and directed operations with a handkerchief bound tightly round the wound. Alerted by the uproar, the shore forts now opened fire on the *Esmeralda*; but the authorities had previously arranged that the British frigate *Hyperion* and the United States ship *Macedonina*, also in the roads, should hoist coloured lights in case of a night attack. Cochrane now had similar lights run up to the mast head of the *Esmeralda*, so confusing the gunners.

In Cochrane's words, 'The whole affair from beginning to end, occupied only quarter of an hour, our loss being thirty wounded, whilst that of the Spaniards was a hundred and sixty, many of whom fell under the cutlasses of the Chilenos before they could stand to arms.' Weak from loss of blood, Cochrane retired to the *O'Higgins* after the capture of the *Esmeralda*, relinquishing command to Guise, who then cut her cables and broke off the action, subsequently giving as his reason that 'the English had broken into her spirit room and were getting drunk, while the Chilenos were disorganized by the plundering'. This was against the orders of Cochrane, who had envisaged a further attack on the rest of the Spanish shipping, and was to cause more bad blood between the two men, briefly reconciled when they led boarding parties from opposite directions and fought side by side on deck. Nevertheless, the cutting out of the seemingly impregnable Spanish flagship was one of the signal achievements of the campaign, and Captain Basil Hall of H.M.S. *Conway*, comments that 'This loss was a death-blow to the Spanish naval force in that quarter of the world; for, although there were still two Spanish frigates and some smaller vessels in the Pacific, they never afterwards ventured to shew themselves, but left Lord Cochrane undisputed master of the coast.'

Although San Martín was prompt with his congratulations, it was not long before he infuriated the touchy Cochrane by declaring that the operation had been jointly planned and claiming a lion's share of the credit for the army. By way of an olive branch he then proposed that the captured frigate should be renamed the *Cochrane*, an honour which Cochrane declined, rechristening the ship the *Valdivia*. This, in turn, upset Captain Guise, who considered himself slighted by being left out of the earlier expedition. Feelings ran so high that Guise and Spry resigned from the squadron and offered their services to San Martín, who did nothing to reduce the temperature by appointing Spry his naval aide-de-camp.

The real bone of contention between the two commanders remained San Martín's refusal to attack the now thoroughly demoralized Spaniards in Lima: far from exploiting the success, he now gave orders for the army to be ferried further up the coast from Ancón to Huacho. An amphibious attack in March 1821 on Pisco,

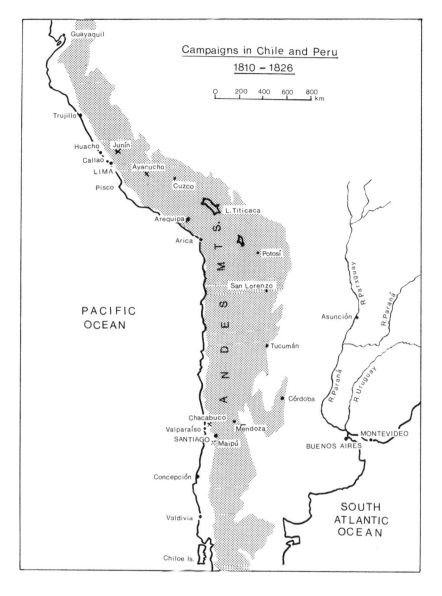

Campaigns in Chile and Peru
1810 – 1826

again in Spanish hands, by 600 men under Colonel Miller, resulted in large gains, but he was brought to a halt when San Martín signed an armistice with the new Viceroy, General La Serna. During the enforced inactivity at Huarás the Chilean army had lost a third of its effectives from fever, and, according to William Bennet Stevenson, 'it became a daily task at the tables of the officers, to drink to "those who fight for the liberty of Peru, not to those who write, *a los que pelean por la libertad del Peru, no los que escriven"* '. San Martín, who was himself ill and had taken up quarters on the schooner *Montezuma* to convalesce, was unshakable:

> The people are asking why I do not march on Lima immediately. I could do it and I would do it now if it were convenient. I do not seek military glory, nor am I ambitious for the title of conqueror of Peru: I only wish to free it from oppression. What good would Lima do me if its inhabitants were hostile politically?

When Cochrane learned of a proposal for extending the armistice for a further sixteen months, following a coup in Madrid and the restoration of the liberal 1812 Constitution, and 'feeling certain that there was something wrong at headquarters', he set sail for Callao, entering the bay on 2 July. This show of strength resulted in the precipitate evacuation of Lima by the Viceroy, La Serna, who withdrew most of his troops into the interior on 6 July, leaving the rest to reinforce the forts of Callao. San Martín inexplicably remained aboard the *Montezuma* and issued no orders for the army to move in, so that the *Cabildo* found it necessary to appeal to Captain Basil Hall of H.M.S. *Conway* for a party of British marines to keep order in the city. When San Martín finally entered Lima it was incognito and by night on the 9th.

Considerable numbers of patriot guerrillas, known as *montoneros* (or 'mountaineers'), were by now fighting behind the lines in the Andes and inflicting significant damage on the royalists; when, instead of lending his support, San Martín decided to quarter his troops in Lima, he appears to have made a major strategic mistake. As it was, San Martín let the opportunity slip through his fingers – final victory in Peru was not to be achieved for another two years by the more resolute action of Simón Bolívar – and, having proclaimed himself 'Protector of Peru', made a series of announcements in bombastic Latin American style, which in retrospect, and in view of the disappointing performance of his government in Lima and the barbaric treatment of the Spanish section of the community, seem rhetorical and empty.

On 4 August, Cochrane, who in common with the squadron which had forced the Spanish capitulation, had been cold-shouldered in the general distribution of commemorative medals, went ashore to ask for payment of the seamen's wages, now a year in arrears, to which San Martín had pledged himself at the start of the expedition. His secretary, W. B. Stevenson, has left an account of the interview with San Martín, which illumines the shabby treatment so often, unfortunately, meted out to the foreign volunteers.

To Cochrane's request, 'San Martín answered, "that he would never pay the Chilean squadron unless it was sold to Peru, and then the payment should be considered as part of the purchase money." To this Lord Cochrane replied, that by such a transaction the squadron of Chile would be transferred to Peru by merely paying what was due to the officers and crews for services done to Peru. San Martín knit his brows, and turning to his two ministers, Garcia and Monteagudo, who were in the room, ordered them to retire; to which his lordship objected, stating that as he was not a master of the Spanish language, he wished them to remain as his interpreters, fearful that some expression, not rightly understood, might be considered offensive. San Martín now turned round to the Admiral, and said, "are you aware, my lord, that I am Protector of Peru?" "No," said his lordship. "I ordered my secretaries to inform you of it," returned San Martín. "That is now unnecessary," said his lordship, "for you have personally informed me: but I sincerely hope that the friendship which has existed between General San Martin and myself will still continue to exist between the Protector of Peru and myself." San Martín, rubbing his hands, said, "I have only to say, that I am protector of Peru!"

'The manner in which this last sentence was expressed roused the admiral, who advancing, said, "then it now becomes me, as the senior officer of Chile, and consequently the representative of the nation, to request the fulfilment of all the promises made to Chile, and the squadron, but first and principally the squadron." San Martín returned – "Chile! Chile! I will never pay a single real to Chile! and as to the squadron, you may take it where you please, and go where you choose: a couple of schooners are quite enough for me: Chile! Chile! *yo nunca pagaré un real a Chile! y en quanto a la esquadra, puede Vd. llevarla donde quiere, e irse quando guste, con un par de goletas me basta a mi;*" and snapped his fingers in the face of the Admiral. On hearing this, Garcia left the room, while Monteagudo walked to the balcony. San Martín paced the room for a short while, and, turning to his lordship, caught his hand, and said, "forget, my lord, what is past!" The admiral, dashing away the tear which surprize and indignation had suffused his eye, replied, "I will, when I can," and immediately left the palace . . .'

In his own *Narrative of Services*, Cochrane adds: 'General San Martín, following me to the staircase, had the temerity to propose to me to follow his example – viz, to break faith with the Chilian Government to which we had both sworn – to abandon the squadron to his interests – and to accept the higher grade of "First Admiral of Peru". I need scarcely say that a proposition so dishonourable was declined; when in a tone of irritation he declared that "he would neither give the seamen their arrears of pay, nor the gratuity he had promised."'

The problems of pay loomed so large that Cochrane now hit on an idea both for paying his men and obtaining possession of the forts of Callao, still in Spanish hands. This was to allow the Spanish commander to evacuate the forts without harassment on payment to the squadron of one third of the large amount of treasure contained there. San Martín, getting wind of the negotiations, at once suspected treachery and made a better offer. In the event, both plans fell to the ground, because at this juncture General Canterac, in Stevenson's words, 'with 3200 men, passed to the southward of Lima – within half-musket shot of the protecting army of Peru, composed of 12,000 – entered the castles of Callao with a convoy of cattle and provisions, where he refreshed and rested his troops for six days, and then retired on the 15th of September, *taking with him the whole of the vast treasure deposited therein by the Limeños*, and leisurely retreating on the north side of Lima.'

San Martín had briefly buried the hatchet and asked for help from the squadron, but to Cochrane's offer to lead the cavalry against the Spanish column in person, he coldly replied, 'I alone am responsible for the liberties of Peru, *yo solo soy responsable de la libertad del Perú*' and calmly retired for his siesta while Canterac's men made good their escape. Miller puts down San Martín's masterly inactivity to jealousy over the possession of the fortresses, but his second-in-command, General Las Heras, and various of his staff were so disgusted as to resign from the Peruvian army.

By mid-September the seamen were so short of food, spirits and clothing, that the ship's company of the *O'Higgins* despatched a letter to their captain, described by Cochrane as being 'somewhat incomprehensible', but 'intended as a farewell complimentary address to myself, previous to the desertion of the flagship':

CAPT CROSBY, Esq.

WE would wish to acquaint you of wot his bean read to us on board of the different C. States ship under his Lordship's Command Concerning the Capture of the *Ismeralda*.

Sir it was thus

the importance of the Service performed by your Lordship to the States by the Capture of the Frigat *Ismeralda*, and the brilliant manner in which this noble enterprize was conducted under your Command on the memorable night of the fift of November, has aurgumented the claims which your previous services gave to the Consideration of the government and those that is Interested in thar cause as well as my present esteem.

All those who partook in the risk and glory of this Interprise deserves also the estermation of thar Companions in the Army, and I enjoy the pleasure of being the organ of thar Sentiments of Admiration Wich so important an action as praduced in the officers and army, Permit me tharfore to express thar sentiments to your Lordship that may be communicated to the Officers and Seamen and troops of the Sqwardon.

Regarding the premium for the Frigat It is to be regretted that the memorey of so herioic an Interprise should be mixed with the painful ideer that blood as been shed in Accomplishment, and we hope that your Lordship and the Gallant Officers and Seamen may be enable to give new days of Glorry to the cause of indispendence

Ship's Company, *O'Higgins*

N.B. – Warre One Single Sentiment his not been fulfilled.

The squadron was now to have 'ocular demonstration that its arrears could be paid'. San Martín had given instructions for large sums of bullion to be loaded into his yacht, the *Sacramento*, for conveyance to Ancón and safekeeping there. Cochrane there and then pursued the yacht and an accompanying merchantman and formally 'seized the treasure, before witnesses'. Part, which he satisfied himself belonged to private individuals, was returned to them, and the balance of 285,000 dollars was applied to payment of the arrears. Accounts of this high-handed transaction were duly forwarded to the Ministry of Marine in Valparaiso, but the furious San Martín condemned it as rank piracy. Relations between the two had now reached a point of no return, and Cochrane shortly afterwards received the Protector's orders to quit Peruvian waters.

He did not immediately return to Valparaiso as instructed by San Martín, but taking the view that the squadron was no longer accountable to the Protector, since he had disowned allegiance to Chile, sailed in pursuit of the Spanish frigates *Prueba* and *Venganza*, which had escaped to the north. It was an adventurous voyage, which took some of the ships as far as California and came near to disaster when the *O'Higgins* sprang a serious leak and was once again saved from sinking by Cochrane's repairing the pumps with his own hands.

Agents of San Martín had, however, meanwhile secured the surrender of both ships, and the *Prueba* was finally discovered hauled in under the guns of Callao and in the command of Cochrane's old opponent, Captain Guise – subsequently to serve with distinction as Admiral of the Peruvian navy and to die in an attack on Guayaquil in 1828. Whatever his personal feelings about San Martín, it was no part of Cochrane's plans to enter into hostilities with Peru; and on 10 May, 1822, he sailed from Callao for the last time for Valparaiso.

After San Martín's resignation in September 1822, following an inconclusive meeting with Bolívar and the rejection of his somewhat eccentric plans for instituting a monarchy with a member of one of the European royal families at its head, one of the first acts of the new Peruvian Congress was to move a belated vote of thanks to Lord Cochrane. Neither he nor San Martín, who retired to Buenos Aires, only to be disowned by his compatriots and to spend the remainder of his life as an impoverished exile in Paris, was to play a further part in the final liberation of Peru, although Miller was to make a perhaps decisive contribution at the Battle of Ayacucho in December 1824 (see page 95).

Cochrane returned briefly to Chile with thoughts of settling on his estate at Quintero, on the coast near Valparaiso, in what he now regarded as his adopted country. It was not to be, since he fell increasingly foul of the government over the perennial problem of back pay for his men, and was at the same time embroiled with the foreign merchants and the British Admiralty over his high-handed methods in dealing with neutral shipping and contraband.

Like that of San Martín, the star of O'Higgins, Supreme Director of Chile, was declining. He, too, with considerably less justification, had been dubbed a tyrant and had aroused bitter opposition among the entrenched landowners because of reformist measures such as the toleration of non-Catholics, an extension of educational and cultural facilities, and a proposal to abolish the *mayorazgos* (or entailed estates).

Cochrane was willy-nilly involved in the march of events. Among

O'Higgins's bitterest opponents was General Ramón Freire – soon to supersede him – who had so courageously supplied Cochrane with troops for the attack on Valdivia. Freire now wrote asking for support in toppling the government; and although Cochrane roundly refused to participate in any plot against his friend O'Higgins, he came under growing suspicion from the authorities and especially from his old antagonist Zenteno at the Ministry of Marine, who lost no opportunity of disbanding the squadron, until only the little *Montezuma* remained under the admiral's command. Cochrane's situation was untenable; he had received a pressing offer from the Emperor of Brazil to continue the struggle for liberation on the other side of the continent; and at this juncture even the elements conspired against him, when the great earthquake of November 1822 demolished the house so lovingly constructed at Quintero.

Since the departure of his wife and children for England in April, 1821, Cochrane's constant companion had been Maria Graham, widowed by the death of her husband while in command of the British frigate *Doris* in Chilean waters and better-known by her later title of Lady Callcott, under which she wrote *Little Arthur's History of England*. With her and a group of his officers, he now decided to take passage to Rio de Janeiro.

Always interested in agricultural and technical improvements, he had earlier imported a lithographic press, the first of its kind in Chile; and, aided by Maria, one of his last tasks was to print a farewell address. In its flowery style, it yields nothing to the pronouncements of his erstwhile companion-in-arms, San Martín.

CHILENOS – MY FELLOW COUNTRYMEN
The common enemy of America has fallen in Chili. Your tricoloured flag waves on the Pacific, secured by our sacrifices. Some internal commotions agitate Chili. It is not my business to investigate their causes, to accelerate or retard their effects; I can only wish that the result may be favourable to the national interest.
CHILENOS. You have expelled from your country the enemies of your independence, do not sully the glorious act by encouraging discord and promoting anarchy – that greatest of all evils. Consult the dignity to which your heroism has raised you, and if you must take any step to secure your national liberty – judge for yourselves – act with prudence – and be guided by reason and justice.
It is now four years since the sacred cause of your independence called me to Chili. I assisted you to gain it. I

have seen it accomplished. It only remains to preserve it. I leave you for a time, in order not to involve myself in matters foreign to my duties, and for other reasons, concerning which I now remain silent, that I may not encourage party spirit.

CHILENOS. You know that independence is purchased at the point of the bayonet. Know also, that liberty is founded on good faith, and on the laws of honour, and that those who infringe upon these, are your only enemies, amongst whom you will never find

COCHRANE

Quintero, Jan. 4th, 1823

V 'SOLDIER LIBERATORS'

THE large northerly area of South America was named by the Spaniards *Tierra Firma*. It included the Captaincy General of Venezuela (or Caracas) to the east, New Granada (present-day Colombia) further west, and also the provinces of Panamá and Darien on the isthmus, and of Veragua in North America. The coastal regions of the Caribbean as far south as the mouth of the Orinoco comprised the famous Spanish Main.

A few weeks before the *porteños* in Buenos Aires declared their 'Provisional Junta, governing for Ferdinand VII', the leading citizens of Caracas had for identical reasons taken a similar step on 19 April, 1810. The newly-arrived Spanish Captain General, Emparán, was compelled to sign away his rights and those of his colleagues of the Royal *Audiencia* on the occasion of a ceremonial meeting of the *Cabildo* (or city council) in the cathedral at Caracas and in the face of a mass demonstration in the main square. The first Venezuelan congress, while still acknowledging loyalty to Ferdinand VII, took a further step towards independence on 2 July, 1811, and in December of that year a constitution was approved, converting the country into a federal republic.

The prime movers, the landed and aristocratic creoles, were by no means universally popular: other towns, such as the royalist stronghold of Coro, and the provinces of Guayana and Maracaibo refused to follow the lead from Caracas; and it was with widespread popular support that the Spanish authorities fought back against the rebellion. To obtain foreign backing for what was obviously destined to be a protracted and bitter struggle, Simón Bolívar, then twenty-six and a colonel in the Junta's army, was despatched to London.

The *Libertador*, in whose service thousands of British soldiers of fortune gave their lives, was born in Caracas in 1783 of an aristocratic creole family with extensive estates near the capital. His father, a member of the dissident group who looked to Miranda, died when Simón was only two-and-a-half and he was thereafter educated by exceptionally gifted tutors, including the poet Andrés Bello and Simón Rodriguez, who did much to awaken the boy's lively mind and accompanied him on trips to Europe. It was a knowledge of the classics, of modern European literature, especially the writings of the French Encyclopaedists, and a deep interest in political theory, acquired in Madrid, Paris and Rome, which stamped Bolívar as a man apart from the other revolutionary leaders in South America.

If, in the end, despite his sweeping military successes, he came to the bitter conclusion that 'For us, America is ungovernable', it was for reasons well put by Irene Nicholson in her illuminating and intuitive book, *The Liberators*: 'The problem . . . was how to achieve a balance between democratic freedoms and a degree of control that would avoid anarchy or at least constant disturbances in the new and largely uneducated countries. It is a problem that has not grown less through the years . . .'

Assessments of Bolívar's capacities as a soldier and tactician run the whole gamut from the uncritical panegyrics of his South American biographers to the blunt statement of his aide, General Ducoudray Holstein, that 'he has never in person commanded a regiment; he has never made a charge of cavalry, nor with a bayonet; on the contrary, he has ever been careful to keep himself out of danger', or the accusation made to his face by one of his staunchest lieutenants, José Antonio Paez: 'I have never lost a battle wherein I acted by myself, or in a separate command, and I have always been defeated when acting in concert with you, and under your orders.'

Whatever his shortcomings (and it makes him less than human to pretend that he had none – he was often both dictatorial and ruthless), the overriding fact remains that he possessed a magnetism and authority which marked him out as the only possible leader. Time and again, and when things were at their blackest, the bickering revolutionary commanders turned to him and pledged their support. And Bolívar surpassed them all in the breadth of his political views, learning from his early mistakes and reverses.

His mission to England was only partially successful in that the Marquess of Wellesley would go no further than a guarantee of help against a French invasion and an offer of mediation with Spain (see page 25); but the visit was of the utmost importance because of his meeting with that veteran champion of an independent Venezuela, Francisco de Miranda (see page 20) and because he became so deeply impressed by British forms of democracy as to be influenced by them in all his subsequent political writings and schemes for the government of South America.

Bolívar sailed back to Venezuela on 20 September, 1810, shortly to be followed by Miranda and later by thousands of British volunteers enlisted by Luis López Méndez, who had accompanied him and who remained in London as the agent of the new regime.

The spirit in which these volunteers flocked to enrol under his banner for a war on the other side of the world had little to do with idealism and has been vividly put by the anonymous author of *Recollections of a Service of Three Years during the War-of-Extermination in the Republics of Venezuela and Columbia*: 'Having been paid off at the conclusion of the late [Napoleonic] war, I had been in England near sixteen months, when this expedition was first made a subject of conversation through the medium of the newspapers. I had found a life of indolence, although varied by the multifarious pleasures of the metropolis, ill suited to one who, for the nine previous years, had been accustomed to the unceasing bustle of active service. I had besides an unconquerable passion for my profession, the rough scenes and continued changes in which accorded with my disposition. I felt miserable when I saw that I was most likely to prolong the life of inactivity I was then leading; and that there was no probability of my being again employed under the glorious flag of England. Nothing, therefore, was more calculated to delight me than the prospect that my services would be acceptable in the reputable cause of Venezuela. I at once made up my mind, and eagerly commenced preparations for the trip; and in total opposition to the wishes of friends, and in spite of their entreaties, commands, or threats, determined at all hazard to persevere.'

Another officer, G. L. Chesterton, who had been retired from Wellington's army 'upon a scanty modicum of half pay', had been looking for employment in all directions, when he fell in with a military friend in the Strand, who promptly took him by the hand and exclaimed: '"Now, my boy, for South America, flags, banners, glory, and riches!"'

Volunteers such as these, encouraged by large promises of pay and promotion to a rank one step above that which they held – or said that they held — in the British army, took ship without any conception of the rigours involved in fighting in the disease-ridden swamps of Guiana, of the jealousy of native-born officers or of the patent inability of the impoverished revolutionary government to meet its financial obligations. Few would ever return to England, and among those who did it became second nature to pen a volume of memoirs, blaming Bolívar as the source of their misfortunes.

There were, of course, men who adjusted to local conditions, became devoted to the Liberator and were handsomely rewarded when his fortunes improved. Among such were Daniel Florence O'Leary, born in Cork, who came to Venezuela as a cornet in Colonel Henry Wilson's Red Hussars, saw service during the campaign in New Granada in 1819 before transferring to Bolívar's staff at the Battle of Carabobo, subsequently remaining his chief aide. His extensive memoirs, running to twenty-nine volumes, have formed the basis for most of the biographies of the Liberator.

Francis Burdett O'Connor, son of an Irish rebel, was another who rendered long and faithful services, eventually joining the staff of General Sucre and entering the service of Bolivia; while Dr Charles Moore of London, of whom Bolívar once said 'my physician is a luxury, not a necessity – the same as my chaplain whom I discharged', after working in military hospitals from 1818 acted as the Liberator's personal surgeon from 1823 to 1828. The loyal services of Lieutenant-Colonel William Ferguson, who gave his life for Bolívar, and of Colonel Belford Wilson are described later.

One of the basic causes of misunderstanding with others, such as Colonel Gustavus Hippisley and the Frenchman Ducoudray Holstein (who had served on Napoleon's staff), was that they expected to fight a gentleman's war in eighteenth-century European style, and this attitude is reflected in their bitter strictures on a disorganized army composed in the main of peasant guerrillas.

Nowhere does this emerge more clearly than in the opening chapters of Hippisley's *Narrative of the Expedition to the Rivers Orinoco and Apuré*. A half-pay cavalry lieutenant, Hippisley was the first to accept the terms of Bolívar's London agent, López Méndez, in May 1817. After his appointment as Colonel he undertook to raise a regiment of hussars, and his first concern was to approach a firm of military outfitters, Messrs. Thompson & Mackintosh (overstocked, like their competitors, with surplus equipment) and to agree the details of uniforms more appropriate to comic opera than the jungles of the Orinoco.

In his own words, 'The established uniform of the regiment was a dark green jacket, with scarlet collar, lapels and cuff, with an ornamented Austrian knot on the arm above; a laced girdle round the waist, and two small gold scaled epaulettes; dark green trousers edged with similar gold lace down the sides, chacco, etc. by way of dress clothing. Undress – dark green jacket, with red cuff and collar, without facings, trimmed with black lacing; dark green foraging cap, with grey overalls, Wellington boots, etc. Crimson sashes, black leather pouch, belts, sabre sash, etc. etc, completed the field or morning uniform.

'A blue camlet cloak, lined with red baize, was the only addition thought necessary for the officer; the whole expense of whose uniform [to be met by the volunteer himself] was under £40 . . .'

These indispensable preliminaries completed, Hippisley proceeded to enlist his men, amounting to forty-four officers and 124 other ranks, including a certain Henry White, senior surgeon to the expedition, who was put in charge of another matter much on Hippisley's mind – the messing arrangements. 'It was proposed by the committee, that each officer should pay into their hands the sum of £14 10s. towards the expenses attending the laying in of wine, spirits, pigs, poultry, etc and every other requisite wanted for the use of the general mess . . .'

In the meantime there was prolonged delay over sailing, the contractors having (with reason) grown uneasy about the Venezuelan government's guarantees. Came the day when the *Emerald* was at last to move off from Blackwall, it was discovered that the perfidious White had embezzled the funds and that the cupboard was bare. He was found, and under pressure 'twelve dozen of good old port, and ten dozen of white wine (a mixture of sherry, lisbon, cape) was sent on board. The pigs had been received, just as the ship was leaving the canal; the poultry, consisting of fowls, ducks, and a few geese, came on board', but of the promised barge with the groceries and preserved meat there was no sign. Instead, 'an officer came on board with the melancholy and distressing information that Mr. White was arrested, and lay at that moment in a spunging house, with no hope of release . . . The surgeon was deaf and callous to all feelings, and like the tortoise, when attacked drew himself under the cover of the impenetrable shell which covered his carcase. Within the walls of the spunging house, he sheltered himself from attacks of every kind . . . unmindful and careless of the miseries he was entailing on forty-five fellow beings, who he was permitting to go to sea . . . without any prospect of relief . . . and purses drained to the last shilling, in aid of the comforts, and even luxuries, which they had all been taught to expect . . .'

Matters went awry from the moment the *Emerald* sailed from England – though the hussars did not fare as badly as a regiment of lancers recruited by a Colonel Skeene, embarked shortly before in the ship *Indian*, which went down with the loss of all hands on the rocks off Ushant. Hippisley was faced with insubordination and mutiny and coldly received by the Portuguese and English authorities, clearly at a loss as to what attitude to take towards the expedition, when he put in for provisions and water at Madeira and Grenada. When he and his men, depleted by desertions in the West Indies, finally made their way two hundred and fifty miles up the Orinoco to Bolívar's headquarters at Angostura (now the town of Ciudad Bolívar), it was to find that the Liberator was fighting in the interior.

After Bolívar's return to Venezuela in 1810 and the declaration of independence in 1811, he took a leading part in the struggle against the Spaniards; but the revolt was a failure and he fled to Curação. In 1813 he fought a successful campaign in New Granada, which he crowned by entering Venezuela and capturing Caracas, only to lose it again in July 1814 after his defeat at the hands of the *llanero* guerrillas under their savage chieftain, José Tomás Boves. In the face of Spanish brutalities, Bolívar issued his famous declaration of a War of Extermination in June 1813:

> The hangmen who call themselves our enemies have violated
> the sacred rights of men and nations . . . But these victims
> shall be avenged, these hangmen exterminated. Our
> vengeance shall rival Spanish ferocity. Our good will is at
> last exhausted; and since our opponents compel us to mortal
> warfare, they shall disappear from America and our land
> shall be purged of the monsters that infest it. Our hate shall
> be inexorable and our war shall be to the death.

From this point the war took on an aspect of unparalleled savagery with atrocities on both sides; and with the despatch from Spain of strong reinforcements under General Pablo Morillo in 1815, most of the revolutionary gains were lost during the following year. After repeated attempts at a come-back, it was not until July 1817 that Bolívar established a secure base for further operations at Angostura.*

Hippisley was not in fact the first British officer to serve with Bolívar. As early as 1813 a Scots adventurer with a suspect knighthood, Sir Gregor McGregor, with a small force of 400 lancers and 200 infantry, had rendered signal services in the capture of Santa Fé (now Bogotá) in New Granada, and later, in 1816, cut to pieces a

---

* Angostura is perhaps better-known for its bitters, extracted from the bark of *Cresparia febrifuga* and once used as a remedy for the dysentery and fever which were to decimate the foreign legionaries.

Spanish army of 2000 at Alacrán near Caracas, shortly afterwards joining forces with General Piar to win the important battle of Juncal.

McGregor, who married a niece of Bolívar and astonished the creoles by habitually dressing in a kilt and having his troops piped into battle, returned to England in 1817 to recruit a force of some six hundred men. After an initial success in capturing Porto Bello on the north coast of Granada, it was surprised by the royalists, and in the words of a contemporary, 'the whole of [them], with the exception of the few killed in the late attack, were thus made prisoners, and immediately marched across the Isthmus to Panamá, where the men, chained two and two together, were employed in filling a swamp near the town, and in cleaning the streets; and the greater part of the officers, to the number of about twenty, were sent to an unhealthy situation on the coast of Darien, where, two months afterwards, under pretence of their having attempted to escape, they were all, with the exception of Major Baldwin, barbarously shot.'

It was, however, on the strength of McGregor's earlier successes and of the heroism of British officers such as Captain Chamberlayne, who conducted a forlorn defence of Cumaná in 1817, finally shooting himself and his wife in the face of the onrushing Spanish, that Bolívar, whose fortunes were then at low ebb, had sent to England for further reinforcements at the suggestion of Ducoudray Holstein.

In the Liberator's absence from his headquarters at Angostura, a little town lost in a tropical forest and washed by the alligator-infested waters of the Orinoco, Hippisley was formally welcomed by General Bermúdez. He almost immediately fell out on a point of etiquette with another of Bolívar's lieutenants, the fiery General Montilla, and was promptly placed under house arrest. This was only the first of a series of quarrels with native officers over precedence, billeting and pay – which was in such a constant state of arrears that the officers had to sell their personal effects to buy food and medicines.

The hussars were at last ferried upstream in large canoes to join Bolívar at San Fernando on the River Apuré, which they found in a state of chaos, the patriot troops having just been routed by the Spanish. Hippisley's men, who had been on the rampage for rum, now ran amuck, and he was entirely unable to contain the mutiny: some under a Major Ferrier were for joining Páez and others for deserting to a rival British contingent, the Red Hussars, under Colonel Henry Wilson. Gathering such troops as remained to him, Hippisley beat a hasty retreat downstream to Angostura and, after an undignified exchange of letters with Bolívar, made his way back to England. With his insistence on etiquette, ceremonial, uniforms and a 'good table', he was not of the stuff of freedom-fighters. Wilson (not to be confused with Colonel Belford Wilson, later to serve Bolívar so loyally) had meanwhile attempted to drive a wedge between General Páez and Bolívar and was dismissed for his pains. It has even been said that he was a spy in the pay of the royalists.

In spite of these disappointments Bolívar did not lose his faith in the fighting qualities of British troops and officers, and when Colonel James English, who had started his military career in the commissariat and come out with Hippisley as a major, suggested that he should round up further volunteers and deserters in the West Indies, the Liberator fell in with the proposal. The wily English, who had had his fill of dirt, disease and slaughter on the Orinoco, next offered to go to London and, for £50 a head and his own promotion to Brigadier-General, to recruit a large contingent for service in South America. Chesterton describes him as 'a man of medium stature with a swarthy complexion, black hair, whiskers, and mustachios, and . . . a person who could assume either a most forbidding or inviting demeanour . . . He proceeded to dilate upon the prospective advantages of the service, and the beauty and fertility of the land of promise.' So persuasive was he that in short time he enlisted some 1,200 men for his British Legion, with its motto of 'Die or conquer'.

With the inducement of a colonelcy, Captain George Elsam, who had been briefly in Angostura, was also authorized to recruit a further thousand men. He set to work with a will and promptly sent off a number of shiploads of equipment and troops, some of them veterans of the Napoleonic wars from Germany, and amounting to seven hundred in all. He was not, however, destined to lead them himself, since he died shortly after returning to Venezuela. Three hundred and fifty of the men subsequently died of malignant fever while on ship from the Apuré to Margarita Island, and one hundred and fifty survivors were placed under the command of Colonel Johannes Uslar, the leader of the Hanoverian detachment.

A good account of the British Legion's subsequent fate is that in *Recollections of a Service* (see page 75). Its author did not, however, like Chesterton, succumb to English's blandishments, but made his way to Margarita Island, off the Venezuelan coast, in command of a

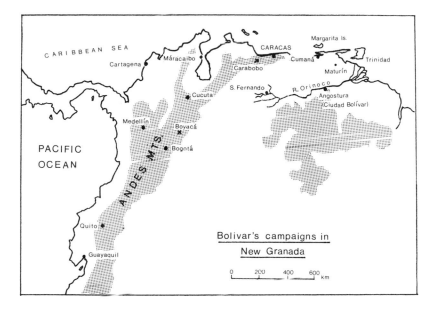

Bolivar's campaigns in
New Granada

ship for a smaller Irish expedition mounted by a Major Beamish, who died during the passage.

On their arrival at the island shortly afterwards, the Legion underwent all the earlier privations of Hippisley's contingent. There was little food and no pay, and from the start officers and men felt that they had been lured to South America under false pretences. Matters were made worse by the open feud between the Governor of Margarita, General Arismendi, and General Urdaneta, whom Bolívar appointed over his head to take command of the Legion.

Nevertheless, the troops were ferried to the mainland and captured the coastal town of Barcelona, east of Caracas, without opposition. There followed the usual disgraceful massacre of prisoners: 'The Spaniards, who had behaved with great pusilanimity, had no sooner surrendered, than the natives, who had accompanied us, began their murderous work; and it was continued without intermission, until every individual of the entire 1300 was despatched. Myself and the whole of the British kept aloof from this spectacle as much as possible . . . I received a severe reprimand, as did my brother officers, and the seamen, for not having taken an active part in the slaughter; Admiral Brion, and subsequently General Urdenetta, both informed us, that as we had entered the service of Venezuela, we were expected to conform to its usages; and in future

81

they insisted on our personal share of putting the prisoners to death. We made no reply; but I believe that all inwardly resolved never to obey any such order.'

General Urdaneta proved incompetent as well as brutal and greedy – appropriating for himself monies and supplies destined for the troops – and failed to grasp the opportunity of engaging a much inferior relief force sent from Caracas. Instead, he ordered the Legion to the strongly fortified town of Cumaná along the coast. The hungry British were spoiling for action, when Urdaneta announced that he was marching them inland.

'A consultation was immediately held by the principal officers of the brigade, and accompanied by the English, they waited upon Urdenetta in a body, and remonstrated with him on the impolicy of his proceedings. They assured him that the men would certainly mutiny . . . After a lengthened consultation, he most reluctantly consented to an attack upon Cumana; but positively declined giving any directions himself. "If it is to be done," said he, "it must rest upon yourself, General English". This was nearly as bad as a direct refusal, as English relished fighting very little . . . At length, with a doleful countenance he agreed . . .'

After heavy loss, the legionaries were on the point of overwhelming the fortifications commanding the town, when to their surprise they heard the bugles sounding a retreat. Despite his pledge, Urdaneta had intervened, and when the troops refused to budge, ordered the retreat in peremptory terms, leaving the survivors exposed to a withering cross-fire. The author of the *Recollections*, whose 'strong silk hat, covered with oiled silk, to withstand the wet' had saved him from a lethal blow with a musket butt, hurried up to English, well to the rear, for orders, 'but he was too much agitated to consider the appeal; and referring me to Colonel Stopford, galloped to the banks of the gulf, and pretending sickness, went immediately on board one of the ships. As nothing could induce him again to take the field, he was never afterwards seen by the army; but sailed to Margarita at the first opportunity, where he some time after caught the yellow fever and died.'

Urdaneta now proceeded with his plan for marching the army over a 9,000 ft. high Cordillera of the Andes to the town of Maturín. In the words of the *Recollections*, 'All descriptions of the dreadful sufferings endured must fall far short of the reality.' The route lay across a series of rivers, 'whose streams were so swollen and currents rendered so strong and rapid by the falls of rain, that in fording them numbers of men, from their excessive debility, were unable to bear up against the force . . . The rush of waters bears down the body with the rapidity of a shot, dashing it in its course against stumps of trees, jutting rocks, and loose stones, until life is extinct, and the sweeping tide is stained with blood.' More than four hundred of the British died at this stage of the march; but worse was to come when they began the ascent of the mountains.

'Their shoes, from being constantly saturated with water, became so enlarged, that they were continually escaping from their feet; and to add to their misery, the surfaces of the mountains were chiefly composed of sharp-pointed stones, resembling in colour broken Scotch granite, but harder . . .' Their lacerated feet were invaded 'by myriads of insects named chegoes . . . These tormenting creatures will penetrate the skin, even when it is unbroken, and breed under it to such an extent, that unless they are speedily removed, the swarm becomes incalculable, and sometimes produces mortification.' On the plains of Maturín the soldiers at first quenched their thirst from the pools of brackish water 'until several of them were found dead at the margin of these receptacles for small alligators and snakes of the most poisonous description.' Others succumbed to 'a species of fish, called the raya, which oftentimes seized their thighs and calves of the legs, and tore large pieces from them, leaving those who survived altogether incapable of further service'.

Maturín had been three times occupied by the Spaniards and razed to the ground, and on reaching its objective the exhausted army found nothing except 'irregular rows of mud-built hovels'. Most of the soldiers were by now suffering from intermittent fever and ague, and the hospital consisted only of 'two square plots of ground, enclosed with mud walls . . . Dirt, disease, and famine were the reward of the services of men who had left their country to embark in the desperate cause of those who now so ill requited them. Many were lodged in the worst hovels of the town, where they were left to perish . . .'

The author of the *Recollections* was one of the fortunate survivors and was later to become one of Bolívar's personal entourage, escorting him down the Orinoco in a canoe, after the victory of Boyacá in August 1819, to Angostura, where the Liberator proclaimed the union of Venezuela and New Granada as the Republic of Gran Colombia. He was also present at Bolívar's meeting with General Morillo in November 1820, when the two agreed on a six months' armistice, and has left a piquant description of the encounter, which took place at the Spanish headquarters near Trujillo:

'After their healths had been successfully proposed by each other, they, as if by mutual desire, arose to embrace, according to the custom of the country; and the men who, for years had been the most inveterate enemies, and had each essayed to surpass his antagonist in the slaughter of their respective countrymen, now hugged and kissed each other in the warmest and apparently most cordial manner . . .

'Finally, each being completely intoxicated, a briezo [toast] was given to the healths of both Generals at once, by their order, and according to the custom the glasses were dashed to pieces on the table, which they then severally mounted again to embrace each other. Unfortunately, their motions not being very steady in a sort of *pas de deux* which they were dancing on the table after the embrace was over, it suddenly gave way, and they abruptly descended to the floor, where they rolled for sometime, until picked up, still embracing each other with the greatest vehemence.

'The chiefs being carried to a bed-chamber, they slept in the same room, and all retired till the next morning, when the second part of this friendly compact was made known.'

Early in 1820, the last of the large-scale British expeditions had arrived in the Caribbean. The so-called Irish Legion was recruited in Dublin through the efforts of a plausible young Irishman, John Devereux. By offering commissions for £1000 – and later for what he could get for them, sometimes as little as £100 – Devereux amassed a fortune of £60,000 and enrolled officers enough for an army of 50,000. 'Meantime,' in the words of the *Recollections*, 'about 2000 men were got together in Dublin, through the medium of glaring hand-bills posted at every convenient spot. Not well-disciplined and seasoned troops, inured to fatigue and danger of every description, like those taken out by General English, but a confused, heterogeneous mass, varying from the peasant fresh from the ploughshare, to the artisan, whose close, sedentary occupation rendered him sickly, and altogether unfit for the active duty of a soldier . . .'

Devereux took good care not to go out with them, but remained at home to enjoy his ill-gotten gains; and when the expedition arrived without warning in Margarita, seven hundred and fifty of its members were at once carried off by yellow fever. The remainder were transported to the Rio Hacha in New Granada, where they fought with considerable bravery under General Montilla, but were soon driven back to the coast by the royalists.

The author of another contemporary memoir, *The Present State of Colombia*, takes up the story. 'Brion and Montilla, who were not accustomed to the management of such turbulent spirits, and neither of them ever manifested any particular partiality for Englishmen, became now very desirous of getting rid of them; and, partly by persuasion, and partly by threats of force, got the greater part of them on board of some English vessels in the harbour, and obliged the captains to convey them to Jamaica . . . they were, in general, a class of persons not wanted in the island; and, after considerable difficulty to determine how to dispose of them, they were at last shipped off, at the expense of the corporation of Kingston, for the British settlements in Canada, and nothing more has been heard of them.' Some hundred of the men were, however, incorporated in the British Legion and they were later to play their part in helping Bolívar to win the crucial battle of Carabobo in 1821.

The episode had a sequel which is pure comic opera. To revert to the *Recollections*, 'some of the persons he had cheated placed [Devereux] in imminent danger of either being arrested or shot. One or two spirited young men challenged him in Dublin, and . . . he escaped privately to Liverpool, where he chartered a coal brig to convey himself and his "staff" . . . to Margarita' in the full expectation of being shot. He was, however, met on board the *Mary* by the author of the *Recollections*, who put his mind at ease. 'This information at once dispelled the cloud which had hung over his countenance,' and Devereux then hastened to unpack his general's dresses, 'all soldered up in tin cases, that the lustre of the lace and bullion might not be diminished by the damp during the voyage.' Arrayed in a sky-blue French field-marshal's uniform, he now set out for a meeting with General Arismendi, but unfortunately paused on the way for his horse to drink from a pool. 'The animal, finding the element cool and comfortable, instantly plunged in up to the knees and, maugre all the efforts of his rider to prevent it, laid himself down and rolled in it, splashing Devereux with mud raked up from the bottom of the stagnant pool and leaving him to wade out at his pleasure.'

Despite the mishap, he proceeded to regale Arismendi with a two-hour speech in English, larded with such phrases as '"Tell 'em, I'll destroy every Spaniard in South America; tell 'em *that*; – say, that all Ireland is up in their cause, in consequence of my representations, – tell 'em *that*;" until the officer getting completely tired, observed, "You must wait till you can tell them yourself, General, for I never talked so much before in my life."'

Although Devereux never actually joined his legion or saw action with it, he has at least one disinterested act to his credit. After the death of General English, his widow arrived in Cucuta in 1821 to claim arrears of pay and a pension from the government. According to Ducoudray Holstein, 'Some evil-minded persons spread a report that she was not the lawful wife of the General; and the Vice-president, Nariño, called on her, with witnesses and interpreter, in order to ascertain the fact.' His attitude was so insulting that Devereux intervened, first writing a letter to Nariño, confirming that Mrs English was in fact the General's wife, and later challenging him to a duel. He was thrown in prison for his pains and kept for six weeks 'in a dark and deep dungeon, where he was confined as a criminal'.

The author of the *Recollections* also remonstrated with Nariño, who 'condescended to load me with every epithet his imagination could suggest at the moment, and concluded by calling me a traitor to the Republic. I remonstrated warmly . . . and the only answer I received was an inkstand, thrown at me by Nariño. Unable to bear this, I seized a small brass rod on which was hung a curtain surrounding his desk, and, before his attendants could prevent it, threw it at him in return. I was then removed to another cell not far from the one occupied by Devereux, and there left to my ruminations.' Both men were later exonerated by Bolívar.

Despite all the chicanery, all the mismanagement and the set-backs, the various British expeditions left Bolívar with a much-needed residue of hardened troops and officers, who were to stand him in good stead during the later phases of the war. After an epic passage of the Andes in 1819, rivalling that of San Martín and his army in Chile, he broke into New Granada and was accompanied by two detachments of foreign troops, the Rifles Battalion under Lieutenant-Colonel Arthur Sandes and the British Legion (sometimes called the Albion Battalion) commanded by Colonel James Rooke.

During this historic campaign it was the heroic charge of the Legion at the Battle of Pántano de Vargas, which, in a desperate situation, drove the royalists from the commanding heights, that made possible the subsequent defeat of the Spaniards at Boyacá, thus sealing the fate of New Granada. Rooke, who had once told Bolívar that he would follow him 'to the mouth of hell if it should be necessary', had an arm amputated and did not survive. The story goes that he seized his severed arm with his good hand, raised it in the air, and shouted '"Long live the fatherland!" To the surgeon's question,

"Which country, England or Ireland?", he replied, "The one which is to give me burial."' Major Mackintosh, who succeeded Rooke in command of the British Legion at the Battle of Boyacá, was promoted by Bolívar on the field of battle.

Such had been the sufferings of the troops during the passage of the Andes that José Enrique Rodó relates of their triumphant entry into Bogotá that 'They came as spectres, and these spectres were those who were strong of body and soul, because the weak remained in the snow, in the torrents on the mountain-tops, where there was no air for the lungs'. A South American writer, Pedro M. Ibañez, adds that 'at the dedication of a column of victory in Bogotá, Bolívar was crowned with laurels by Señorita Dolores Vargas. Bolívar replied in a happy speech, first taking off the crown and putting it on Santander and then Anzoátegui and finally held it towards the Rifles Battalion, saying "Those soldier liberators are the men who deserve these laurels."'

After the six months' armistice of 25 November, 1820, and the subsequent recall of General Morillo to Spain, the days of the royalists were evidently numbered. Although the war lingered on for another two years, the *coup de grace* was the Battle of Carabobo, fought on 24 June, 1821. It is vividly described by an officer of the British Legion, quoted by William Pilling in *The Emancipation of South America*; although his account, written from the standpoint of an active participant, perhaps does less than justice to Bolívar's role in directing the overall tactics.

'We halted at dusk on the 23rd at the foot of the ridge. The rain fell in torrents all night and reminded us of the night before Waterloo. Next morning the sky was cloudless when we stood to arms, and presently Bolívar sent us the order to advance. We were moving to get round the enemy's right flank, where his guns and infantry were partly hidden by trees and broken ground. Bolívar after reconnoitring ordered us to attack by a deep ravine, between the Spanish infantry and artillery. The enemy's guns opened fire and our men began to fall. Meanwhile the Bravos de Apure had advanced within pistol-shot of the Spaniards, and received such a murderous volley from 3000 muskets that they broke and fled back in disorder upon us.

'It was a critical moment, but we managed to keep our ground till the fugitives had got through our ranks back into the ravine, and then our grenadier company, gallantly led by Captain Minchin, formed up and poured in their fire upon the Spaniards, who were only a few paces from them. Checked by this volley, the enemy fell back a little, while our men, pressing eagerly on, formed and delivered their fire, company after company.

'Receding before our fire and the long line of British bayonets, the Spaniards fell back to the position from which they had rushed in pursuit of the Apure Bravos. But from thence they kept up a tremendous fire upon us, which we returned as rapidly as we could. As they outnumbered us in the ratio of four to one, and were strongly posted and supported by guns, we waited for reinforcements before storming their position. Not a man, however, came to help us, and after an hour passed in this manner our ammunition failed. It then really seemed to be all over with us. We tried, as best we could, to make signals of our distress; the men kept springing their ramrods, and Colonel Thomas Ferrier, our commanding officer, apprized General Paez of our situation, and called on him to get up a supply of cartridges. It came at last, but by this time many of our officers and men had fallen, and among them Colonel Ferrier. You may imagine we were not long in breaking open the ammunition-boxes; the men numbered off anew, and after delivering a couple of volleys we prepared to charge. At this moment our cavalry, passing as before by our right flank, charged with General Paez at their head. They went on very gallantly, but soon came galloping back and passed again to our rear, without having done any execution on the enemy, while they had themselves suffered considerably.

'Why Bolívar at this time, and indeed during the period since our first advance, sent us no support, I have never been able to guess. Whatever the motive, it is certain that the second and third divisions of the army quietly looked on while we were being slaughtered, and made no attempt to help us. The curses of our men were loud and deep, but seeing that they must not expect any help, they made up their minds to carry the enemy's position, or perish. Out of nine hundred men we had not above six hundred left; Captain Scott, who succeeded Colonel Ferrier, had fallen, and had bequeathed the command to Captain Minchin; and the colours of the regiment had seven times changed hands, and had been literally cut to ribands, and dyed with the blood of the gallant fellows who carried them. But, in spite of all this, the word was passed to charge with the bayonet, and on we went, keeping our line as steady as on a parade day, and with a loud "hurrah" we were upon them. I must do the Spaniards justice to say they met us gallantly, and the struggle was for a brief time fierce, and the event doubtful. But the bayonet in the hands of British soldiers, more especially such a forlorn hope as we were, is irresistible. The Spaniards, five to one as they were, began to give ground, and at last broke and fled.

'Then it was, and not till then, that two companies of the Tiradores came up to our help, and our cavalry, hitherto of little use, fiercely pursued the retreating enemy. What followed I tell you on hearsay from others, for I was now stretched on the field with two balls through my body. I know, however, that the famous battalion of royalists called "Valence", under their gallant colonel Don Tomas García, covered the enemy's retreat, and was never broken. Again and again this noble regiment turned sullenly on its pursuers, and successfully repulsed the attacks of the cavalry and infantry of the third division of our army, which now for the first time left their secure position and pursued the Spaniards.

'As for our regiment, it had been too severely handled to join in the pursuit with much vigour. Two men out of every three were killed or wounded. Besides Colonel Ferrier, Lieutenant-Colonel Day, Captain Scott, Lieutenants Church, Houston, Newel, Stanley, and others, were killed; and Capts. Minchin and Smith, Lieutenants Hubble, Matthew, Hand, Talbot, and others, were wounded. The remains of the corps passed before the Liberator with trailed arms at double quick, and received with a cheer, but without halting, his words, "Salvadores de mi patria!" – Saviours of my country!'

According to official figures the royalists, between dead and wounded, lost 2900 of their 5100 effectives, but in all probability the casualties were nearer 3500 – a very high figure in a war where the opposing armies often numbered no more than a thousand men and the addition of another few hundred might well mean the difference between victory or defeat.

Bolívar entered Caracas in triumph on 29 June, 1821; and the Constitution of Gran Colombia was adopted at Cúcuta during the following August and September, with Bolívar as President and General Santander as Vice-President.

His next objective was Quito, across the Andes to the west and now part of modern Ecuador. After a hard-fought campaign, in which the Rifles Battalion under Captain Wright and Colonel Sandes once again played a leading part, the city fell in May 1822. Guayaquil, further to the west, had already been occupied by one of the ablest of Bolívar's lieutenants, General José Antonio Sucre, advancing from Peru with an army which included the battle-tried Albions. The Liberator was now poised to expel the Spaniards from their last stronghold in South America, the mountain fastness of Upper Peru.

VI MILLER OF PERU

IN February 1824 General Miller, as he had now become, was on sick leave in Chile at the warm baths of Colina in the Andes. 'The arduous service, upon the unhealthy coast, in which he had been engaged, again brought on a serious attack of ague and fever. This disease was rendered worse by the breaking out of an old wound in the thigh, which occasioned violent and unceasing pain . . .' At this juncture he received the dramatic news that the Peruvian Congress had dissolved itself, naming Bolívar dictator.

Since the abdication of San Martín and the departure of Lord Cochrane in the autumn of 1822, little progress had been made in expelling the Spaniards from Peru. The French-born General Canterac, with an army of 5000, threatened Lima from the north-east; General Valdéz's army of 3000 effectively controlled the Puertos Intermedios in the coastal region of Arequipa in the south; while the die-hard royalist, General Olañeta, with another army of 3000, was in secure possession of the famous silver-mining region of Potosí in the depths of Upper Peru (now Bolivia) to the east of the Andes. Further Spanish garrisons were scattered around important towns such as La Paz and Cuzco, where the Viceroy, La Serna, had established his new seat.

The inhabitants of Lima were war-weary and disillusioned with their liberators; and neither a daring raid by Miller and his Peruvian Legion in the Spanish-occupied area to the south nor the appointment of the brilliant General Sucre as supreme military chief had prevented the temporary occupation of Lima by General Canterac. When Bolívar arrived in person, it was to find that the garrison of Callao, in long arrears of pay, had mutinied and turned over the fortresses to the royalists, so that he was compelled to set up his headquarters at Huarás, to the north.

It was to Huarás that Miller immediately repaired, taking passage from Valparaiso in the brig of war, *El Congreso*. After a running battle with a Spanish privateer, during which he narrowly avoided capture, he arrived in Huarás in May to offer his services to the Liberator.

Of their first interview, Miller writes: 'His eyes are dark and penetrating, but generally downcast, or turned askance when he speaks . . . the expression of the countenance is careworn, lowering, and sometimes rather fierce. His temper, spoilt by adulation, is fiery and capricious. His opinions of men and things are variable. He is rather prone to personal abuse, but makes ample amends to those who will put up with it . . . Speaking so well as he does, it is not wonderful that he should be more fond of listening to himself talk than of hearing others . . . Disinterested in the extreme with regard to pecuniary affairs, he is insatiably covetous of fame . . .'

As to Miller, Bolívar evidently had no reservations, since at the end of their interview he named him *commandante-general* of the Peruvian cavalry.

Bolívar's first objective was to seek out and destroy the army of General Canterac, then encamped near the Lake of Reyes, one of the sources of the Amazon, and rather to the east of the great divide of the Andes; and Miller was ordered to prepare the way by crossing the mountains, taking command of the tough *montonero* guerrillas in the region and establishing hidden supply dumps in the galleries of abandoned silver mines along the route.

'Some of these depots were established within the line of country nominally possessed by the royalists. That near Pachia, and on the same bank of the Rio Grande, was only eight leagues from Tarma. The entrance of the cave was in the perpendicular side of a cliff fifty or sixty feet from the ground and as many from the top. The only way to get up was by a rope fixed in the cave, and by notches cut in the rock to give foot-hold. Indian corn, salt, charqui (jerked beef), potatoes, and barley, were hoisted up by means of the rope. A few men were sufficient to defend these cavern-depots against any numbers. It often happened that when the montoneros advanced, these depots were left exposed; but the royalists were not always aware of the exact situation, and entertained no suspicion that supplies had been accumulated.'

The army proper, commanded by Bolívar in person, with Sucre as his chief of staff, began its advance across the mountains in July; and in the words of Miller's *Memoirs*, 'The shelving ledges, which afforded the only foothold on the rugged sides of the Andes, are so narrow, as to render the passage indescribably harassing. The troops could advance only one by one. The single file was sometimes lengthened out to an amazing extent by the *Mal Pasos* formed by deep gullies or breaks in the tracks, by projecting rocks, or by numerous waterfalls; all of which required great caution, and much time to pass in safety.'

It was of particular importance that the cavalry – the *gauchos* of the Argentine Pampas, the *guasos* of Chile and the *llaneros* of Colombia, described by Miller as 'perhaps the best horsemen in the world', should arrive in good condition. 'Each man', therefore, 'had, besides the mule on which he rode, a led horse, to be mounted only in sight of the enemy . . . The *lasso* was used, as upon every other occasion, with great adroitness. Fastened round the neck of the led horse, it was shortened or lengthened as the tortuous windings of the ascent or descent required . . .'

Miller, whose special charge this was, adds: 'It [often] became necessary for every man to dismount, and to lead the two animals in his charge, to avoid going astray, or tumbling down the most frightful precipices. But the utmost precautions did not always prevent the corps from losing their way. Sometimes men, at the head of a battalion, would continue to follow the windings of a deafening torrent, instead of turning abruptly to the right or left, up some rocky acclivity, over which lay their proper course . . . One party was frequently heard hallooing from an apparently fathomless ravine, to their comrades passing over some high projecting summit, to know if they were going right. These would answer with their trumpets; but it often occurred that both parties had lost their road. The frequent sound of trumpets along the broken line; the shouting of officers to their men at a distance; the neighing of horses, and the braying of mules, both men and animals being alike anxious to reach a place of rest, produced a strange and fearful concert, echoed, in the darkness of the night, from the horrid solitudes of the Andes.'

Another hazard faced by the advancing patriots was *surumpi* or snow-blindness. Miller describes how 'A pimple forms in the eye-ball, and causes an itching prickling pain, as though needles were continually piercing it. The temporary loss of sight is occasioned by the impossibility of opening the eyelids for a single moment, the smallest ray of light being absolutely insupportable. The only relief is a poultice of snow, but as that melts away the tortures return.' Later in the campaign, a whole division was blinded in this way, and the long files of sightless soldiers were led into the nearest village by Indian guides, but not before a hundred stragglers had been lost along the line.

It seems that General Canterac was suffering from over-confidence after the easy Spanish victories in the Puertos Intermedios and was quite unprepared for the emergence of the patriot army on the tableland, 12,000 feet up and to the east of the high Andes, in a state ready for combat. On the morning of 5 August Bolívar's troops, skirting the western shore of the great Lake of Reyes, suddenly caught sight of the enemy in retreat towards the plains of Junin on the opposite side.

Threatened by a patriot advance to the south of the lake, Canterac put himself at the head of his cavalry and charged. Miller, who had been ordered to attack the royalist flank with two hundred and fifty of the Peruvian cavalry, was impeded by swampy ground and, together with the troops under General Necochea, faced a full frontal attack. The result was a total patriot rout; but the Spanish cavalry, instead of keeping formation, dispersed in pursuit and were caught in the rear by an unbroken Peruvian squadron. 'The patriots now used their lances with such effect, that the boasted cavalry of the Spanish was soon in a state of disgraceful flight, and pursued to the very bayonets of their infantry.' The royalists were not pursued and had not suffered large loss, but there were desertions on a massive scale during the subsequent retreat, and when Canterac reached Cuzco it was with only 5000 of his original 9000 men.

Only a handful of the surviving members of the Albion Battalion and a few other foreigners took part in the battle, but among the casualties was an old companion in arms of Miller, Lieutenant-Colonel Sowersby. 'He had received two lance wounds, neither of which were then thought dangerous; yet his countenance was marked with melancholy thoughtfulness, and tinged with a wild and wandering expression, that bespoke approaching death. At first he hardly noticed his friend, but, after a short pause, he grasped his hand, and said, with a faltering voice, "My dear Miller, we took arms in this cause almost on the same day. We have often fought side by side. You have witnessed my conduct. You are my oldest and best friend in this service. I am too feeble to say much. You see what is likely to happen . . ." Poor Sowersby, who had fought under the banners of Napoleon at Borodino, and who had survived the horrors of the Russian campaign, died on the following day at Carhuamayo, in his twenty-ninth year.'

The news of Junín came at a critical juncture for the Spaniards, since the Viceroy, La Serna, had shortly before despatched a punitive expedition under General Valdéz against the ultra royalist, Olañeta, who regarded his colleagues as little less than dangerous radicals. Valdéz was immediately recalled and 'by one of those extraordinary marches for which he was celebrated' succeeded in joining Canterac near Cuzco. La Serna now took personal command of the combined force of 13,000, which greatly outnumbered the patriot army.

Bolívar had meanwhile departed to Lima to organize reinforcements, leaving Sucre in supreme command, but with instructions to avoid engaging the enemy during the approaching rainy season. Towards the end of September Sucre summoned a council of war, attended by Generals La Mar, Lara and Miller. They were uneasy about the build-up of the Spanish army, but hesitant about disobeying Bolívar's explicit orders. In the upshot Miller convinced the others that 'the most *prudent* plan was to act *boldly* on the offensive' and, together with an able German officer, Colonel Althaus, was despatched with a squadron of cavalry and some *montonero* irregulars, to reconnoitre the royalist dispositions. During the next weeks they soon verified that Valdéz had joined the Viceroy and that the combined Spanish force was about to resume the offensive.

Miller was seldom more than within riding distance of the advancing Spaniards, and on one occasion the hut where he had rested for the night was occupied by the Viceroy half-an-hour afterwards. On another, 'Miller took off his clothes for the first time for a fortnight, and retired to rest. The royalist General Valdéz, never deficient in courtesy, and who had a few days before sent Miller a box of Havannah cigars, now despatched a company of infantry to procure him the society of his opponent.'

Betrayed by the village priest, Miller abandoned his mount, 'considered the best horse in the army', and made his escape over the mountains on foot, 'followed by the yelling Indians, increasing in numbers at every hut near which they passed'. Althaus was less fortunate. Some time before he had appropriated a 'milk-white mule' used for carrying the host to Mass. Surprised by the Indians, he was transferring the saddle from the mule to his charger, when the horse took fright and galloped off. Miller makes the dry comment that 'It is probable they would have taken his life, but that his clerical figure led them to imagine that he was the regimental chaplain, an illusion which Althaus took no pains to dispel.'

On 6 November Miller rejoined the patriot army, which until then had been in ignorance of the close proximity of the royalists. For the next month, amidst driving rain, the two armies marched and countermarched amongst the steep wooded defiles and along flooded watercourses, jockeying for position and offering and declining battle. To discourage desertions, 'The royalists avoided entering villages, and kept as much as possible along the ridges of the mountains . . .

'The vice-king, for the same reason, was averse to sending detachments in search of cattle, for, on such occasions, a number of men were sure to desert. The consequence of this system was, that, during the rapid advance of the royalists, they suffered more than the patriots from want of provisions; so that, on the 3rd, they were reduced to eat the flesh of their horses, mules, and asses.'

When night fell on 8 December the opposing armies at last found themselves face to face, with the Spaniards occupying the heights of Condorcunca (an Indian term, meaning 'worthy of the condor') and the smaller patriot army drawn up in the plain below. In the words of the *Memoirs*, 'The night of the 8th was one of deep and anxious interest. A battle was inevitable on the following day, and that battle was to decide the destinies of South America. The patriots were aware that they had to contend with twice their numbers; and that nothing but a decisive victory could save them and their country from ignominious servitude. The patriot *soldier* might indeed expect to escape with *life*, reduced to the condition of a slave; but with the patriot generals and officers, it was only a choice between death and victory. They knew full well what would be the cruel policy of the Spaniards if they proved victorious.'

The morning of 9 December, 1824, on which the decisive battle of Ayacucho was to be fought, dawned chill but sunny; and at 9 a.m. the Viceroy led his men down the hill. General Sucre rode along his lines, reminding the troops 'That upon the efforts of that day depended the fate of South America'. By this time the royalists were forming up in the plain, and the patriot General Córdova was ordered to the attack with his division of infantry, supported by two regiments of cavalry. Holding his hat above his head and exclaiming '"*Adelante, paso de Vencedores!*" ("On with the steps of conquerors!")', he led the onslaught in person. The Spaniards at first held firm, and for three or four minutes the issue was in doubt, but at this juncture a headlong charge of the Colombian cavalry drove the royalists back to the heights above. Their line broke; the slaughter began; and the Viceroy was wounded and taken prisoner. But the battle was by no means over.

At first light General Valdéz, making a large detour, had taken up positions on the left flank of the patriot army, sheltered by a ravine. He now opened a destructive fire from his four field pieces, obliging two battalions of La Mar's Peruvian division to fall back; and a

Colombian battalion sent to their aid was unable to stem their flight. The Spaniards now crossed the ravine in pursuit. At this critical moment Miller and his hussars charged the advancing Spaniards, driving them back across the ravine, taking Valdéz's artillery and forcing back his troops to the heights of Condorcunca. Here, the royalists attempted to rally, but shortly before sunset Canterac rode down to Sucre's tent and surrendered. It was an Englishman, Captain George Brown who finally raised the Colombian flag on the summit.

The Battle of Ayacucho had cost the Spaniards some 2000 killed and wounded as against 1000 on the patriot side, but more important, it effectively brought to an end the centuries-long domination of South America by the Spaniards, since in the subsequent capitulation La Serna agreed to withdraw all his troops from the former Viceroyalty of Peru.

Miller's *Memoirs* supply some interesting human sidelights. 'The men, of one squadron, and all the officers of a royalist cavalry regiment wore silver helmets. These became the objects of the particular attention of the patriot soldiers, during the pursuit. Some had the presence of mind to save themselves, by throwing off their helmets, which, like the golden apples of Hippomenes, did not fail to arrest the progress of their pursuers. These silver baits proved as irresistible to the patriot soldiers, as the apples of Atalanta. In a few hours every silver helmet had changed, not exactly heads, but owners; for all were broken up and stowed away in the valises of the captors.'

About midnight Miller called to pay his respects to the captured Viceroy, whom he found 'sitting on a bench, and leaning against the mud wall of the hut. A feeble glimmering from the wick of a small earthen lamp threw just enough light around to render visible his features, which were shaded by his white hair, still partially clotted with blood from the wound he had received . . . The viceroy was the first to speak, and holding out his hand, said, "*You*, general, we all know full well: we have always considered you as a *personal* friend, notwithstanding all the mischief you have done and the state of alarm in which you have so repeatedly kept us."' La Serna's wound had not even been dressed, and Miller immediately sent for a surgeon. 'When the wound was dressed, Miller, in tendering his further services, told the viceroy, that the only refreshment he had it in his power to offer was a little tea, which he happened to have with him, and which he believed no other person in the army could supply . . . When the tea was brought, the

Scenes in contemporary Peru. *Above* Travellers setting out from Tarija.
Below A night's lodging at the Curate's house.

Antonio José de Sucre.

Gregor, Cazique of Poyais ('Sir Gregor McGregor').

Lancers of the Plains of Apuré.

Simón Bolívar.

A natural bridge in the High Andes.

Below The High Andes – 'One party was frequently heard hallooing to their comrades passing over some high projecting summit'.

venerable viceroy drank it with eagerness, and was perhaps more grateful for this seasonable relief than for any kindness or favour he had ever received.'

Canterac took up his quarters for the night in Miller's hut. 'They laid themselves down upon the earthen floor, where it was difficult to find a dry spot, as the rain pelted through several parts of the roof.' The defeated general was in a high state of excitement and kept repeating, ' "General Miller – General Miller – all this appears to be a dream! (*ésto parece sueño!*) how strange is the fortune of war! Who would have said twenty-four hours ago, that I should have been your guest? but it cannot be helped: the harassing war is now over, and, to tell the truth, we were all heartily tired of it." '

Next morning, 'General Miller saw a Spanish officer approaching his quarters in company with General Sucre. The royalist, a small spare person with a slight inclination to stoop, wore a broad-brimmed hat of Vicuña beaver, a coarse grey surtout, and long brown worsted leggings. When he came near, his keen eyes sparkled and enlivened a sunburnt, weather-beaten, but highly-interesting countenance. Before Sucre had time to introduce him, he ran forward a few paces and embraced Miller, saying, "I know who you are – I am Valdez: – you and me cannot be but friends." Then turning to Sucre, he added, "This Miller has often kept us upon the move. They called *me* active, but *he* was like a wizard (*bruxo*), here, there, and every where, without our ever being able to penetrate his designs, ascertain his numbers, or find out what he was about, until he dealt out some sly blow (*hasta que nos habia pegado algun chasco*)." '

There remained a couple of pockets of Spanish resistance: General Olañeta, who still had some 2000 troops at his disposal, refused to accept the terms of the surrender, as did General Rodil, firmly in occupation of Callao. In March of the following year, Miller, who had meanwhile been appointed governor of the Department of Puno in Upper Peru, was instructed by Sucre to move against Olañeta. 'General Miller was at this time confined to his bed in consequence of the inflammation of an old wound in the side, brought on by over riding when visiting some of the provinces of the department he governed. Fortunately at La Paz (a distance of fifty-four leagues) an English surgeon resided. He was sent for, and upon his arrival at Puno made an incision in his side which stopped the coming mortification, and the general recovered.' Miller nevertheless remained so weak that he was carried on a litter at the head of his men; but the expedition proved unnecessary, since on arriving at Potosí it was to find that Olañeta's troops had mutinied and murdered him.

Rodil, supported by ships of the Spanish navy, held out in Callao for almost another year, assaulted from the sea by Cochrane's erstwhile opponent, Captain Guise, now Admiral of Peru, who fought a brilliant action against the much more heavily gunned Spanish ships, and from the land by a four thousand-strong army, part Colombian, part Peruvian. In the face of famine and pestilence, he finally surrendered on 19 January, 1826.

'Thus,' in the oratorical periods of the *Memoirs*, 'the heroic constancy and perseverance of the patriots, surpassed by no people in ancient or modern times, were crowned with ultimate and complete success throughout South America. The blood-stained standard which Pizarro had planted three hundred years before was trailed in the dust; and the last link of the chain, that but lately bound seventeen millions of Americans to the tottering monarchy of Spain, was finally broken.'

Bolívar attempted to impose Constitutions on Upper Peru – renamed Bolivia in his honour – and on Peru proper.* Like his other grandiose schemes for a Gran Colombia and a South American Confederation, they were later suspended; and shortly before his death in 1830 he left a bitter political testament – prophetic in view of what has transpired:

> I have arrived at only a few sure conclusions: 1. For us, America is ungovernable. 2. He who serves a revolution ploughs the sea. 3. The only thing we can do in America is to emigrate. 4. This country will eventually fall into the hands of the unbridled mob, and will proceed to almost imperceptible tyrannies of all complexions and races. 5. Devoured as we are by every kind of crime and annihilated by ferocity, Europeans will not go to the trouble of conquering us. 6. If it were possible for any part of the world to revert to primordial chaos, that would be America's final state.

---

* The draft Constitution for Bolivia was, incidentally, delivered into Sucre's hands by two British aides, Colonel William Ferguson and Captain Belford Wilson, a son of Sir Robert Wilson of Peninsular War fame, who had covered the 1800 miles from Lima across the High Andes in nineteen days. The devoted Ferguson was later stabbed to death when protecting Bolívar against a group of would-be assassins who entered his bedroom in the presidential palace at Bogota in September 1828.

Miller, whose health had been badly affected by the numerous wounds received in action, resigned his post in October 1825 and was awarded a sum of 20,000 dollars (about £4000) by a grateful government. He also received a letter from Bolívar, acknowledging 'the intrepidity and tact which so much contributed to the victory' and testifying to the fact that he had 'never taken part in any of the factions which have agitated Peru'.

Riding the 1700 miles overland from Potosí, he arrived in Buenos Aires in January 1826, eight years to the day from his departure for Chile. After seventeen years in England and a spell as British Commissioner in the Sandwich Islands, he returned to duty with the Peruvian Army in 1851, dying ten years later. His body was embalmed by the President's physicians, who extracted two bullets and counted the marks of no less than twenty-two wounds.

VII 'INDEPENDENCE OR DEATH!'

IN November 1822, that stormy petrel, Admiral Cochrane, by now thoroughly 'annoyed by the ingratitude with which my services were requited in Chili', received a missive in polished French from the Brazilian representative in Buenos Aires. It reads, in part:

> MILORD,
>   Brazil, a power of the first rank has become a new empire, and independent nation under the legitimate heir of the monarchy, Pedro the Great, its august defender.
>   It is on his orders – and in virtue of ministerial despatches, which I have just received from Monseigneur Joseph Bonifacio de Andrada e Silva, Minister of the Interior and of Foreign Affairs of Brazil, dated September 13 last – that I have the honour of addressing to you this letter; in which Your Grace is invited – on behalf of the Government of Brazil – to accept the service of the Brazilian nation; and I am duly authorized to offer you rank and grade in no way inferior to that which you hold under the Republic . . .

This was shortly followed by an even more pressing invitation: *'Venez, milord, l'honneur vous invite – la gloire vous appelle. Venez – donner à nos armes navales cet ordre merveilleux et discipline incomparable de puissante Albion.'*

'On mature consideration', Cochrane duly replied:

> Sir,
>   The war in the Pacific having been happily terminated by the total destruction of the Spanish naval force, I am, of course, free for the crusade of liberty in any other quarter of the globe.
>   I confess, however, that I had not hitherto directed my attention to the Brazils; considering that the struggle for the liberties of Greece – the most oppressed of modern states – afforded the fairest opportunity for enterprise and exertion.
>   I have to-day tendered my ultimate resignation to the Government of Chili, and am not aware at the moment that any material delay will be necessary, previous to my setting off, by way of Cape Horn, for Rio de Janeiro . . .

On 13 March, 1823, the chartered brig *Colonel Allen*, in which he had embarked from Valparaiso with the now inseparable Maria Graham and ten trusted officers of the Chilean squadron, anchored at Rio.

When General Junot had marched a French army into Lisbon in November 1807, prior to the onset of the Peninsular War proper, the Prince Regent, John, together with his mad mother and an entourage of about a thousand, had set sail for Brazil under the protection of the British navy. They were warmly received; and John had promptly set to work to redress grievances of the sort which so rankled in Spanish America by enlarging the judiciary, encouraging industry, and founding a national bank, a military academy and cultural institutes. Most important of all, he ended the Portuguese trade monopoly by opening the country's ports to friendly nations, a step with the most profound repercussions for the future of Brazil.

After his mother's death, John VI signed an edict in December 1815 making the colony a kingship within the Portuguese empire. However, the ruling Junta in Lisbon, though liberal in its policies at home, was determined to retain the overseas empire at any cost; and when John returned home in April 1821, he was unable to prevent it from undoing most of his colonial reforms. In the absence of three quarters of the Brazilian deputies, the Lisbon Côrtes condemned the opening of Brazilian ports and made nonsense of Brazil's dominion status by decreeing the abolition of the chancery court, the treasury and the newly-established tribunals. To give teeth to these measures it was further decreed that the Portuguese and Brazilian armies should be amalgamated, thus making it possible to send Portuguese reinforcements to Brazil. Independent governors, under direct control from Lisbon, were at the same time appointed to the different provinces.

On leaving Brazil Dom John had left his son as regent, with the advice 'If Brazil demands independence, grant it, but put the crown upon your own head'. Dom Pedro, who was more of a colonial than a European and has been characterized as 'a very democratic-mannered son of a divine-right father', took this advice to heart, but his position was not made easier by the presence in Brazil of two fundamentally opposed factions.

Apart from the 3,600,000 slaves, who accounted for two thirds of the population but were without political influence, the whites were divided between Brazilians of Portuguese descent, who owned the large estates and had traditionally occupied most of the positions of authority, and more recent arrivals engaged in commerce and industry. Both parties were opposed to any going back on Dom John's *carta regia* of 1808, establishing free trade, which would have spelled financial ruin; but whereas the new arrivals or Absolutists, who depended on the slave trade to solve their labour problems and were also opposed to the growing British share in the country's trade, favoured an absolute monarchy under Dom Pedro, with the crown united to Portugal by dynastic ties, the Brazilian party, or Patriots, leaned towards a completely independent constitutional monarchy. Although Dom Pedro was by upbringing and by the nature of his position as Absolutist, it was primarily with the support of the Patriots that he was to succeed in expelling the Portuguese and to establish his authority over the whole huge country.

In the face of Portuguese intransigence. Brazil edged steadily nearer outright independence during the summer of 1822. On 13 May, petitioned by the Municipality of Rio de Janeiro, Dom Pedro assumed the title of 'Perpetual Protector and Defender of Brazil' and took the final step at the insistence of his prime minister, José Bonifácio de Andrada, and of his wife, Leopoldina, who had declared 'The apple is ripe; pick it now, or it will rot'. On the margin of the Ypiranga River near São Paulo, he ripped off the Portuguese insignia from his uniform, shortly afterwards appearing in the Theatre at Rio with the famous *grito de Ypiranga* – 'Independence or death!' – emblazoned on his arm. He was crowned 'Constitutional Emperor of Brazil' on 12 October following.

It was one thing to declare independence and another to secure the evacuation of Portuguese troops from the northern provinces. General Madeira, firmly in possession of Bahía with an army of 3000 regulars and 2000 militia, refused to embark his troops without the sanction of the Lisbon Côrtes. A patriot expedition of some 8000 men proved no match for the well-trained Portuguese regulars, and it was in these circumstances that the appeal for help was despatched to Cochrane.

'During the interim preceding his arrival,' to quote from the contemporary *History of Brazil* by John Armitage, 'the greatest activity succeeded to the inertness formerly apparent in the dock-yard. A voluntary subscription for the re-inforcement of the Navy was entered into with unexampled enthusiasm; all the unemployed vessels of the Government were fitted out for war; and the only seventy-four whose timbers were judged to be sound, was in a manner re-built. It was, however, found utterly impossible to equip these vessels with native seamen, the coasting trade having been hitherto carried on exclusively by Portuguese; and orders were consequently sent to Felisberto Brant, who had been appointed Brazilian Chargé d'Affaires in London, to engage a number of officers and seamen, on terms highly advantageous to the parties. The Military establishment was also augmented, and on the 8th of January a Decree was issued for the organisation of a battalion of foreigners.'

On his arrival in Rio de Janeiro, Cochrane was at once given an audience by Dom Pedro, who accompanied him on a visit of inspection to the ships the following day. With some of them he 'was much pleased, as demonstrative of the exertions which must have been made within a short time to get them into such creditable condition'. He had few complaints of his intended flagship, the *Pedro Primeiro*, rated as a seventy-four, although in fact she mounted only sixty-four guns – and, in fact, she was to prove more than a match in Cochrane's expert hands for anything the Portuguese could send against her. 'Another showy vessel was the *Maria da Gloria* – a North American clipper; a class of vessels in those days little calculated to do substantial service, being built of unseasoned wood, and badly fastened . . . As a redeeming feature, she was commanded by a Frenchman, Captain Beaurepaire, who had contrived to rally round him some of his own countrymen, mingled with native Brazilians – in which he displayed considerable tact to free himself from the unpromising groups elsewhere to be selected from.'

The other crews, Cochrane describes as 'of very questionable description – consisting of the worst class of Portuguese, with whom the Brazilian portion of the men had an evident disinclination to mingle . . . the marines were so much gentlemen that they considered themselves degraded by cleaning their own berths, and had demanded and obtained attendants to wait on them! whilst they could only be punished for offences by their own officers!' It also struck him as an anomaly that 'Not having as yet had experience of political party in the Empire . . . Portuguese should be employed in such numbers to fight their own countrymen, though I afterwards became but too well acquainted with the cause of a proceeding at the time beyond my comprehension.'

There remained certain preliminaries to settle before he hoisted his flag. The Minister of Marine, Luiz de Cunha Moreira, began by offering the 'pay of an admiral of the Portuguese service, – notoriously the worst paid in the world'. After heated argument,

Cochrane gained acceptable terms for himself and the officers who had accompanied him from Chile; but worse was to follow when it emerged that he was being offered the position of Junior Admiral under the orders of two senior ranking officers of the Board of Admiralty. Cochrane at once resorted to José Bonifácio de Andrada and 'begged of him to take back his commission, about which I would hold no further parley'.

'This step was evidently unexpected, for, lowering his tone, Bonifacio assured me that "good faith was the peculiar characteristic of the Brazilian administration"; and to prove this, he had to announce to me that a Cabinet Council had resolved that the newly created honour of "First Admiral of Brazil" should be conferred on me, with the pay and emoluments of Chili, as stipulated by the Consul at Buenos Ayres.'

Thus mollified, Cochrane put to sea on 3 April, 1823, with the four serviceable ships at his disposal: the flagship, the *Pedro Primeiro*, Captain Crosbie; the *Piranga*, Captain Jowett; the *Maria da Gloria*, Captain Beaurepaire; and the *Liberal*, Captain Garcão. They were accompanied by two fire-ships, the *Guarani* and *Real* and later joined by the *Nitheroy*, under the command of another Englishman, Captain Taylor. His orders were to proceed with 'such vessels as he shall judge proper to the port of Bahia, to institute a rigorous blockade, destroying or capturing whatever Portuguese force he may fall in with – doing all possible damage to the enemies of the Empire, it being left to the discretion of the said Admiral to act as he shall deem advantageous . . .'

Having sailed 800 miles up the coast, the squadron sighted a Portuguese fleet of thirteen sail, including one ship of the line and five frigates, near Bahía on 4 May. 'Regularly to attack a more numerous and better trained squadron with our small force, manned by undisciplined and – as had been ascertained on the voyage – disaffected crews, was out of the question. On board the flag-ship there was only a hundred and sixty English and American seamen, the remainder consisting of the vagabondage of the capital, with a hundred and thirty black marines, just emancipated from slavery . . .' Nevertheless, Cochrane spotted an opening in the enemy line and took in the flagship, firing into the frigates and cutting off the four to the rear. 'I could have kept the others at bay, and no doubt have crippled all in a position to render them assistance. To my astonishment the signals were disregarded . . . no efforts were made to second my operations.' On top of this, it was now discovered that 'two Portuguese seamen who had been stationed to hand up powder, were not only withholding it, but had made prisoners of the powder boys who came to obtain it! This would have been serious but for the promptitude of Captain Grenfell, who, rushing upon the men, dragged them on deck; but to continue the action under such circumstances was not to be thought of . . .'

Having safely disengaged the *Pedro Primeiro*, Cochrane vented his indignation on the Prime Minister in Rio: the sails were rotten; the cartridges unfit for service, and he was 'obliged to cut up every flag and ensign that could be spared, so as to prevent the men's arms being blown off while working the guns'; six pounds of powder would not 'throw our shells more than a thousand yards, instead of double that distance'; whilst, worst of all, the crew of the *Real* were *'on the point of carrying that vessel into the enemy's squadron for delivering her up!'* In short, his conclusion was that one half of the squadron was necessary to watch over the other.

It has been said of Lord Cochrane that, among his naval contemporaries, only Nelson displayed an equal spirit of aggression. On the one occasion when the two met, at Palermo, Nelson bade him: 'Never mind manoeuvres, always go at them.' It is characteristic of him that, in a situation of apparently hopeless inferiority, he should now have proceeded to the attack without waiting for support from Rio.

Having set up a base at Moro São Paulo down the coast for the fitting out of fire-ships in anticipation of a full scale attack, he transferred all the reliable seamen from the other ships to the *Pedro Primeiro* and the *Maria da Gloria* and began a blockade of Bahía. Meanwhile, the Portuguese Admiral, though 'in a state of consternation on learning that the fireships were nearly equipped', made no serious attempt to deploy his fleet, and instead the authorities resorted to a war of words:

> The conduct of Lord Cochrane verberates in our ears –
> examine his conduct in the Pacific, and observe that he lost
> all . . .

> It is only the *Pedro Primeiro* that is manned with the
> adventurous foreigners, so that we shall fall on the 74, and
> by beating her decide the business of Brazil . . .

> The usurper who rules in the Capital thinks that, reaching
> the bar with the squadron of his imaginary Empire, we
> should be attacked on all sides, and compelled to make a
> shameful capitulation. How much you are mistaken –

new-born monster! We have abundant force at our disposal; but in the meantime we must overthrow the plans of the enterprising Cochrane, and wait the result of maritime prowess.

Cochrane was meanwhile finding difficulty in assembling crews for his fire-ships and was unwilling for the operation to go off at half-cock, as had happened at the Basque Roads in 1809 and at Callao in 1821. He therefore decided, as a preliminary, to take the *Pedro Primeiro* up the nine miles of river 'on the first dark night' and to reconnoitre the position of the Portuguese fleet.

Having discovered that the Portuguese admiral and his senior officers were to be ashore for a ball on 12 June, 'As soon as it became dark, we proceeded up the river, but unfortunately, when within hail of the outermost ship, the wind failed, and the tide soon after turning, our plan of attack was rendered abortive; determined, however, to complete the reconnaisance, we threaded our way amongst the outermost vessels, but dark as was the night – the presence of a strange ship under sail was discovered – and some beat to quarters, hailing to know what ship that was? The reply being "an English vessel", satisfied them, so that our investigation was made unmolested. The chief object thus accomplished, we succeeded in dropping out with the ebb tide, now rapidly running, and were enabled to steady our course stern-foremost with the stream anchor adrag, whereby we reached our former position off the mouth of the river.'

His irruption caused consternation in Bahía. '"What", exclaimed the Portuguese admiral, interrupted at the height of the festivities, "Lord Cochrane's line-of-battle ship in the very midst of our fleet! Impossible – no large ship can have come up in the dark!" The newspapers immediately changed tone: "In the last few days we have witnessed in this city a most doleful spectacle that must touch the heart of even the most insensible. A panic terror has seized on all men's minds – the city will be left without protectors – and families, whose fathers are obliged to fly, will be left orphans – a prey to the invaders."'

Cochrane, completely outgunned by the Portuguese fleet and out-numbered by the 3000 troops on shore, stepped up the war of nerves by despatching letters to the Junta, General Madeira and the Portuguese Admiral, calling for the departure of the ships and troops to save civilian casualties – a monstrous piece of bluff, since, as he notes in his *Narrative of Services*, 'my mode of carrying on warfare . . . as the Portuguese families afterwards found, both at Bahia and elsewhere, was to protect the defenceless and unoffending'. However, the letters produced their intended effect; and on 2 July a huge convoy emerged from the mouth of the river.

It consisted of the *Dom João*, 74; *Constitução*, 50; *Perola*, 44; *Princeza Real*, 28; *Calypso*, 22; *Regeneração*, 26; *Activa*, 22; *Doz de Fevereiro*, 26; *Audaz*, 20; *S. Gaulter*, 26; *Principe do Brazil*, 26; *Restauração*, 26; *Canceição*, 8; with between sixty and seventy merchant vessels, crammed with Portuguese families and their property, and transports laden with troops.

Once the armada was in open water, the smaller ships of Cochrane's squadron fell on the rearmost merchantmen, 'disabling their main and mizen masts, so as to render it difficult for them to sail otherwise than before the wind, which would carry them back to the Brazilian coast, and ordering them back to Bahia'. Cochrane himself was after bigger game and set sail alone in the *Pedro Primeiro* after the thirteen warships and the transports. On the morning of 4 July, the whole Portuguese fleet put about and gave chase, pursuing the *Pedro Primeiro* inshore. Smartly out-manoeuvred, the squadron then 'resumed its position in the van of the convoy, to which we immediately gave chase as before, and as soon as night set in, dashed in amongst them, firing right and left till the nearest ships brought to, when they were boarded – the topmasts cut away – the rigging disabled – the arms thrown overboard – and the officers compelled to give their *parole* not to serve against Brazil until regularly exchanged – an event not likely to happen.'

At dusk on the 5th some half-dozen large transports were seen to crowd on sail and to detach themselves from the main convoy. The *Pedro Primeiro* caught up with them next morning. As Cochrane had suspected, they were crammed with troops, and the ships were successively 'boarded and disabled, so far as was consistent with not leaving them positive wrecks on the water; for with my single ship, to have made prisoners of so numerous a body of troops was manifestly impossible'.

At this point the brig *Bahia* hove in sight, and her commander, Captain Haydon, was instructed to escort four of the captured vessels to Pernambuco. In a letter to the President of the province, requesting humane treatment of the prisoners, Cochrane added: 'If we can come in, permit me to observe, that it would be conducive to the health of my crew to have ready a supply of fresh provisions and fruits, especially lemons and oranges. I hope you will excuse my freedom in mentioning these things, as the health of my men is as conducive to the interests of the empire as are the ships of war themselves.' Martinet as he was, it was concern such as this, as well as the insistence that his sailors should be properly paid, that won him their unflinching devotion.

The *Pedro Primeiro* meanwhile chased the main squadron across the equator, but while tacking to deliver a broadside in latitude 5 North, her mainsail split and the pursuit was discontinued. Of the original sixty or seventy ships of the convoy, only thirteen escaped, they were pursued across the Atlantic by Captain Taylor, who took over in the *Nitheroy* and destroyed a further four in the mouth of the Tagus under the guns of the *Dom João VI*.

Cochrane's next target was the large provinces north of Bahía, which the troops on the captured transports had been destined to reinforce. Arriving in the River Maranhão on 26 July opposite the city of Maranham, he promptly hoisted Portuguese colours, justifying this habitual ploy as 'a fiction held justifiable in war, and, indeed necessary under our peculiar circumstances, as having only a single ship to reduce a province'.

The authorities, who were expecting reinforcements, immediately sent off a brig of war with despatches and congratulations on the safe arrival of the supposed Portuguese ship. The *Don Miguel's* captain, Francisco Garção, was at once made prisoner on boarding the *Pedro Primeiro*, but offered his release and that of his ship if he would carry sealed letters to the governor and Junta. 'He was duly impressed by the relation of an imaginary number of vessels of war in the offing, accompanied by transports filled with troops, which the superior sailing of the flagship had enabled her to outstrip. Captain Garção being a seaman and well able to judge as to the sailing qualities of the *Pedro Primeiro*, was easily impressed by this story, and returned to the city with intelligence of an irresistible force about to disembark for its reduction.'

Cochrane admits to 'some compunction at this off-hand sketch of an imaginary fleet and army', but 'The sensation caused by the evacuation of Bahia gave probability to my representations, and added to the despondency of the Portuguese, so that the *ruse* was completely successful.' Garção returned almost at once with an offer of conditional surrender; but this was not enough for Cochrane, who entered the river, 'never before navigated by a line-of-battle ship', and anchored abreast of the fort. Next day, 27 July, 1823, the

Junta and bishop came aboard and agreed to submit uncondition-
ally, 'though not without subsequent hesitation, which was dispelled by firing a shot over the town, whereupon a flag of truce was
sent off, and all demands were complied with'. Captain Grenfell
then went ashore with a party of marines and hoisted the Brazilian
colours over the fort.

Forceful action was now essential before the deception was discovered. Cochrane accordingly issued a proclamation in his most
florid style:

> THE FIRST ADMIRAL OF BRAZIL TO THE INHABITANTS
> OF MARANHAM
> The auspicious day has arrived on which the worthy and
> public-spirited inhabitants of Maranham have it in their
> power at once to declare the independence of their country,
> and their adherence to their patriotic monarch, Pedro
> Primeiro, whose protection has afforded them the glorious
> privilege of freedom. . .
> Taking the necessary oaths, and the election of civil
> government are acts which must be deliberately performed,
> and for this, the 1st of August is selected. Citizens! let us
> proceed gravely and methodically, without tumult, haste, or
> confusion, and let the act be accomplished in a manner
> worthy the approbation of His Imperial Majesty, and which
> shall give no cause for regret, and leave no room for
> amendment . . .

For obvious reasons it was important to get rid of the Portuguese
troops, 'for, three days having now elapsed without any appearance of my reputed forces, there was some fear that they might
attempt to recover their former position'. The necessary ships were
quickly assembled in the harbour; but sizable contingents, supported by the militia, refused to go on board, and it was only after
Captain Crosbie had been sent ashore with a large party of marines
to disarm the refractory troops that the transfer was finally effected
without bloodshed. For the next fortnight they lay offshore in the
dawning realization that they had been tricked into surrender, and
the flotilla finally sailed for Lisbon on 20 August.

The political situation, which Cochrane next attempted to resolve
in equally bluff and clear-cut manner, proved to be considerably
less straightforward. The Portuguese authorities 'had filled the
gaols with respectable Brazilian citizens', who were not unnatur-
ally determined to get their own back. Cochrane decreed a more
popular government; elections were forthwith held on 8 August,

and the first act of the new regime was to address a letter to the Emperor in terms no less flowery than his own:

'What was our joy when unexpectedly we saw the *Pedro Primeiro* summoning our port. Oh, 26th of July, 1823! Thrice happy day, thou wilt be as conspicuous in the annals of our province, as the sentiments of gratitude and respect inspired by the illustrious admiral sent to our aid by the best and most amiable of monarchs will be deeply engraven on our hearts and on those of our posterity. Yes! august Sire! the wisdom, prudence and gentle manners of Lord Cochrane have contributed still more to the happy issue of our political difficulties than even the fear of his force. To anchor in our port – to proclaim independence – to administer the oaths of obedience to your Majesty – to suspend hostilities throughout the province – to provide proper government – to bring the troops of the country into the town, but only in sufficient numbers to ensure order and tranquillity – to pen the communications between the interior and the capital – to provide it with necessaries – and to restore navigation and commerce to their pristine state – all this, Sire, was the work of a few days . . .'

Only the northernmost province of Pará, in itself, as Cochrane remarks, larger in area than Britain and France combined, now remained in Portuguese hands. After his successes at Bahía and Maranham, he decided that there was nothing to be lost by trying the same stratagem again. The problem was that he had only one ship, the *Pedro Primeiro*, at his disposal. He therefore commandeered the captured brig *Don Miguel*, renaming her the *Maranhão*, and sent her north under Captain (later Admiral) Grenfell. His instructions were to browbeat the authorities into submission, and for this purpose he was armed with a letter from Cochrane, dated as from the *Pedro Primeiro* at the mouth of the Amazon and representing that resistance was useless. In his briefing for the operation, Cochrane added a terse footnote: 'You will perceive that my intentions are to effect by your means, objects *which would otherwise require an expedition . . .'*

With a force of less than a hundred men, Grenfell carried out these instructions to the letter, incorporating Pará in the empire 'without a dissentient voice – save that of the Portuguese commandant'. The only casualty was Grenfell himself, who was severely stabbed by a would-be assassin after the ruse had been discovered. A Provisional Junta was set up, and an attempt to unseat it was summarily quelled by landing a party from the *Maranhão* and shooting five of the ringleaders.

Lord Cochrane's campaigns
in Brazil

R. Amazon

Pará (Belem)

PARÁ

Maranham (São Luis)

MARANHÃO

Ceará (Fortaleza)

CEARÁ

PARAIBA

PERNAMBUCO

Pernambuco
(Recife)

BAHÍA

Bahia (Salvador)

ATLANTIC
OCEAN

MINAS GERAIS

São Paulo
RIO DE JANEIRO

0   200   400   600
km

In Maranham, Cochrane's experiment in instant democracy was meanwhile running into difficulties, and he was pained to note that 'The Junta of Maranham, indeed, appeared to have no other object than to shew how liberty suddenly acquired could degenerate into despotism'. Having dismissed all the existing officials, the Junta proceeded to fill the vacant posts with 'their own friends, relations and dependents' and next brought in large numbers of irregulars to harry the remaining Portuguese. 'It appeared, moreover, that the Junta and their friends owed large sums of money to some of the more wealthy and influential Portuguese, and that they intended to get rid of their debts, by the expulsion of their creditors.'

Cochrane had already written to José Bonifácio de Andrada 'to

111

suggest most respectfully to His Imperial Majesty my opinion that it would greatly conduce to the peace and prosperity of this province, if some able and honourable person should be sent to take the chief authority'. To this, Andrada contented himself by replying that he was sure the problems would vanish as conditions became more stable and that 'Meanwhile your Excellency – being no less a politician than a warrior, and enjoying to the utmost the confidence of His Imperial Majesty – is fully empowered to adopt whatever means your judgment may suggest to facilitate the important objects of your commission.'

Matters came to a head on 14 September, when the native troops ran amuck, plundering the houses of the Portuguese, deposing the General-at-arms and replacing him by their own nominee, Luis Salgado. Cochrane at once informed Salgado that he was unacceptable and wrote to the Junta, 'threatening to act in a decisive manner, if these disgraceful scenes were not instantly put an end to, pointing out to them that, as they were the chief proprietors of houses and stores, so they would be the greatest sufferers from anarchy'. Having restored order and decreed new elections for 20 October, he announced his own departure in the *Pedro Primeiro* for Pará, 'well knowing that a belief in her speedy return to Maranham would have a salutary influence in maintaining public peace'. He had, however, had his fill of Maranham and its factious politicians and in fact set sail for Rio.

During this first phase of his service for Brazil, within seven months and without loss of a single man or ship, he had neutralized a powerful Portuguese army, defeated a large fleet in the face of odds which would have deterred anyone but himself from making the attempt, and liberated an entire sub-continent. Superb seaman and strategist as he was, it is perhaps to expect too much that he should also have installed stable political regimes in the conquered territories.

Even before Cochrane's return to the capital, Dom Pedro had acknowledged these signal services by conferring upon him the title of Marquess of Maranhão, and the General Assembly had concurred by recording a vote of thanks in the name of the nation. The honour was accepted on his behalf on 12 October by Lady Cochrane, who had arrived unexpectedly in Rio in the interim, and the ceremony is described by Maria Graham in her *Journal of a Voyage to Brazil*: 'This is the Emperor's birthday, and the first anniversary of the coronation. I was curious to see the court of Brazil; so I rose early and dressed myself, and went to the royal chapel . . .

Contemporary engraving of Rio de Janeiro.

The Slave Market at Rio de Janeiro.

Far left Dom Pedro I of Brazil.

Left Lady Cochrane.

Right Admiral Brown in old age.

Below left The Palace of San Cristovão,
near Rio de Janeiro.

Below Naval encounter between Admirals
Brown and Norton; the *Nitheroy*, *República*
and *25 de Mayo*.

J. G. de Francia, Dictator of Paraguay.

'I reached the inner room where the ladies were, just as the Emperor had, with a most pleasing compliment, announced to Lady Cochrane that she was Marchioness of Maranham; for that he had made her husband Marquis, and had conferred on him the highest degree of the order of the Cruceiro . . .

'I should do wrong not to mention the ladies of the court. My partial eyes preferred my pretty countrywoman the new Marchioness . . .'

Maria Graham had settled in a cottage near the house which the government had assigned to Cochrane on his first arrival. She had since been in constant correspondence with him; and behind her honied phrases there lurk heated feelings. Of Lady Cochrane's sudden arrival, another contemporary writes that 'she is making war in grand style and has divided Rio society into two camps, one in her favour and the other against her; the first is captained by her and the other by Maria Graham. They are rival queens and have caused much scandal.'

This was not Lady Cochrane's first appearance in Rio de Janeiro, and her earlier visit in 1822 had caused an equal stir. After a number of adventures in Chile and Peru, during one of which she had been stabbed by a royalist agent at Cochrane's country estate near Valparaiso and in the course of a subsequent journey over the Andes to deliver despatches had again narrowly escaped death at the hands of an assassin, she had struck up a bizarre friendship with Doña Angela de la Pezuela, the wife of the deposed Peruvian viceroy.

The two sailed together on the British frigate *Andromache*, Lady Cochrane on a visit to England and Doña Angela en route for Spain, completing the first leg of their journeys at Rio de Janeiro. They were put up at the Fonda Inglesa, only to find that one of their fellow guests was the Marqués de Valle Umbroso, an envoy from the new Viceroy, General La Serna, to the Madrid court, who had fallen into the hands of the Buenos Airean patriots and been put ashore at Rio.

The Marqués at once moved out, only to spot the irrepressible couple at the theatre next night and to compile an indignant report: 'The first thing we saw was Doña Angela Zevallos de Pezuela, in the embroidered uniform of a Spanish general, prominently seated in a box with her friend and travelling companion, the wife of Cochrane: that same Cochrane who, with the insurgent General José de San Martín, has largely wrested from the Spanish monarchy the vast and opulent dominion of Peru, which your Majesty entrusted to Don Joaquin de la Pezuela, husband of Doña Angela . . .

'If the Spaniards were moved to anger by the sight of these two women together, the Portuguese were much diverted. The Prince Regent, who now noticed the audience looking up at the couple, went to the edge of his box with the Princess on his arm to share the general amusement. Doña Angela, shameless as she was, could not face the ironical laughter of the onlookers and withdrew to the interior of the box as the performance started, so hiding her embarrassment.'

At the present juncture, Maria Graham, having secured the position of governess to Dom Pedro's small daughter, prudently withdrew to England before taking up her duties, but was to return before long – to be pressed into service by Cochrane as an ambassadress in his dealings with the rebels in Pernambuco.

In addition to creating Cochrane Marquess of Maranhão, Dom Pedro had intended to confer on him a large estate. That the proposal ran into immediate opposition from the General Assembly on the grounds that it was arbitrary and undemocratic, was symptomatic of a deepening political crisis. It was precipitated by the Andrada brothers who introduced a measure for the expulsion of all native-born Portuguese judged hostile to the Empire. The Absolutists, who regarded this as a backhand onslaught on themselves, now succeeded in overturning the Andradas and initiating policies favourable to the Portuguese. The Andradas retaliated by attacking both the government and, in veiled terms, the Emperor himself.

Dom Pedro's response was Cromwellian. Putting himself at the head of his army, he rode into Rio, ringed the chamber with guns and sent in a brigadier with an order for its immediate dissolution. Two of the Andrada brothers were arrested on the staircase, and José Bonifácio at his house. All three were then transferred to a vessel in the port and transported to France without more ado. Dom Pedro then proceeded to solve the vexed question of a new constitution by announcing that he would draft it himself. At this point Cochrane, unabashed by his experiences in Maranham, proffered some well-meant advice, suggesting that it was put into effect *even before the sailing of the next packet for Europe'*.

> As no monarch is more happy, or more truly powerful than the limited monarch of England, surrounded by a free people, enriched by that industry which the security of property by means of just laws never fails to create – if Your Majesty were to decree that the English constitution, in its most perfect practical form . . . shall be the model for the Government of Brazil . . . it would excite the sympathy of

powerful states abroad, and the firm allegiance of the
Brazilian people to Your Majesty's throne...

Since Cochrane himself had left England after an unavailing struggle against the corruption rife in the ruling Tory party, his advice
seems a little odd; nevertheless, it was taken in good part, if not
acted on – although a guarantee based on the English *Habeas Corpus*
act was, in fact, incorporated in the new constitution promulgated
on 25 March, 1824.

'Meanwhile, Lord Cochrane himself,' in Armitage's words,
'remained in Rio, patiently waiting the adjudication of his prizes;
and, as a succession of captures were still coming in from the coast
of Portugal, whither Captain Taylor had followed the Portuguese,
the officers and crews of the squadron were led to form the most
flattering hopes. The result, however, did not equal their anticipa-
tions. The prizes had been guaranteed to the squadron previous to
its sailing, but the object of the expedition was now attained, and
His Majesty, under the influence of his Royalist Counsellors, manifested but little eagerness in fulfilling the engagements entered into
during the ministry of the Andradas. He was anxious, in the first
instance, to avoid giving offence to his Portuguese subjects; and, in
the second, by delaying condemnation of the sequestered vessels
and property, to facilitate a peace with the mother country.'

A series of fulminating letters on the subject of prizes and the
seamen's pay was met by evasions of the sort which had earlier
embittered Cochrane's relations with San Martín and the Chileans,
the Prize Court, for example, refusing the squadron's claims on the
grounds that the captures had been made, not in foreign territory,
but in an integral part of the mother country. Armitage describes
how the vessels 'were in the meantime delivered up by an order of
the government, to the charge of the Inspector of the Arsenal, and
by him again to individuals, who, being in no way responsible for
the property on board, allowed it to be carried off by night with the
utmost impunity'. Injustice reached its high water mark when
Captain Taylor was sentenced to six months imprisonment and
ordered to forfeit *double* the amount of his prize money to the
original owners, while Captain Grenfell was not only docked of
prize money, but faced a court martial over the conduct of his
single-handed capture of Pará!

When Cochrane took up the cudgels on behalf of his men and the
Ministry of Marine attempted to buy him off with a bribe, his
contemptuous reply was that 'His Majesty had already conferred

honours upon me quite equal to my merits – and that the greatest personal favour he could bestow, was, to urge on the speedy adjudication of prizes, so that the officers and seamen might reap the reward decreed by the Emperor's own authority'. And even he was subjected to personal slights. His ships were ordered to sea without his knowledge, while the official gazette took to describing him merely as 'Commander of the Naval Forces in the port of Rio'. Matters came to a head when, on 4 June, 1824, he received a visit from Madame Bonpland, the wife of a French botanist, who informed him that his house was surrounded and that, under pretext of a naval review, his flagship was to be searched next morning for illegally secreted treasure.

As Cochrane tells the story: 'I clambered over my garden fence as the only practicable way to the stables, selected a horse, and not-withstanding the lateness of the hour, proceeded to St. Christoval, the country palace of the Emperor, where, on my arrival, I demanded to see His Majesty. The request being refused by the gentleman in waiting, in such a way as to confirm the statement of Madame Bonpland – I dared him to refuse me admission at his peril; adding that "the matter upon which I had come was fraught with grave consequences to His Majesty and the Empire." "But," said he, "His Majesty has retired to bed long ago." "No matter," replied I, "in bed, or not in bed, I demand to see him, in virtue of my privilege of access to him at all times, and if you refuse to concede permission – look to the consequences."

'His Majesty was not, however, asleep, and the royal chamber being close at hand, he recognized my voice in the altercation with the attendant. Hastily coming out of his apartments in a *dishabille* which, under ordinary circumstances, would have been inconsistent, he asked – "What could have brought me there at that time of night?" My reply was – "that understanding that the troops ordered for a review were destined to proceed to the flagship in search of supposed treasure, I had come to request His Majesty immediately to appoint confidential persons to accompany me on board, when the key of every chest in the ship should be placed in their hands, and every place thrown open to their inspection; but that if any of his anti-Brazilian Administration ventured to board the ship in perpetration of the contemplated insult, they would certainly be regarded as pirates, and treated as such". Adding at the same time – "Depend upon it, that they are not more my enemies, than the enemies of Your Majesty and the Empire, and an intrusion so unwarrantable, the officers and crew are bound to resist." "Well," replied His Majesty, "you seem to be apprised of everything, but the plot is not mine; being – as far as I am concerned – convinced that no money would be found more than we already know of from yourself."

'I then entreated His Majesty to take such steps for my justification as would be satisfactory to the public. "There is no necessity for any," replied he; "but how to dispense with the review is the puzzle – I will be ill in the morning – so go home, and think no more of the matter. I give you my word your flag shall not be outraged by the contemplated proceeding."

'. . . The Emperor kept his word, and in the night was taken suddenly ill. As His Majesty was really beloved by his Brazilian subjects, all the native respectability of Rio was early next day on its way to the palace to inquire after the Royal health, and, ordering my carriage, I also proceeded to the palace, lest my absence might appear singular . . . On catching my eye, His Majesty burst into a fit of uncontrollable laughter, in which I as heartily joined; the bystanders, from the gravity of their countenances, evidently considering that both had taken leave of their senses. The Ministers looked astounded, but said nothing – His Majesty kept his secret, and I was silent.'

In the face of the government's refusal to pay prize money or even to meet the squadron's arrears of pay, Cochrane now began threatening to resign. In view of what he and his men had achieved, the evasions over pay entirely justified the stream of blistering letters which he directed to the Ministry of Marine and the Emperor. The withholding of prizes was a more complicated issue and was not, as Cochrane assumed at the time, entirely dictated by the half-hearted attitude of the Absolutist government to Brazilian independence and the desire of some of its members to return to the Portuguese fold.

During 1824 and 1825 Dom Pedro was engaged in intricate negotiations to end the war with Portugal and to obtain foreign recognition of Brazil's *de facto* independence. Great Britain was centrally involved, because, while wishing to maintain the commercial treaty with Brazil, Canning and his ministers were equally anxious to avoid a breach with their oldest ally, Portugal. Largely through the efforts of the British mediator, Charles Stuart, a formula was finally agreed; and with the greatest reluctance the Lisbon court acknowledged the independence of the colony, but only on condition that Brazil paid a large indemnity and made restitution of prizes. In the circumstances the Brazilian government's hesitation to hand over the prizes to its own squadron is understandable – although in breach of its earlier agreement with Cochrane.

Pending the outcome of these delicate negotiations, a new crisis calling for Cochrane's further services had arisen in the northern province of Pernambuco, between Bahía and Maranham. Originally colonized by the Dutch, Pernambuco and its inhabitants had traditionally displayed a lively spirit of independence. Its elected president, the young Manoel Carvalho Paes de Andrada, objected to Dom Pedro's arbitrary dissolution of the Assembly and had come to the conclusion that to be a colony of either Portugal or Rio was equally unacceptable, thereupon declaring independence and inviting the other northern provinces to form a 'Confederation of the Equator'.

It seems that the Portuguese party in Rio was half-persuaded that a revolt in Pernambuco might facilitate a Portuguese invasion; but if his Absolutist ministers dragged their heels, Dom Pedro was convinced of the need for drastic action and, swallowing his pride, applied to Cochrane, who as a last resort had just proffered his resignation.

Despite this ultimatum, the first suggestion of the Ministry of Marine was that he should round up his seamen and 'use my influence with them *to re-enter without payment*'. Out of loyalty to the Emperor, for whom he always retained a personal regard, Cochrane went through the motions of complying with the Ministry's order, then penned the dryest of memos: '. . . I ordered a commissioned officer to visit the different rendezvous which the seamen frequent, and endeavour to prevail on them to re-enter . . . It appears, however, that it will be difficult to prevail on them to engage again in the service, without some explicit declaration made public on the part of the Imperial Government, stating what they have to expect for the past, and to anticipate for the future . . .'

The difficulty was resolved by the Emperor's personal guarantee that 200,000 *milreis* (about £50,000) would at once be advanced in part payment of prize money. Although far short of what was owing, this was duly distributed among the men, enabling them at least to meet their debts to the tavern keepers 'clamorous for payment'; and the squadron put to sea on 2 August, landing 1200 troops under General Lima down the coast before proceeding to the city of Pernambuco (now known as Recife).

'His Lordship did not, it must be owned,' writes Armitage, 'proceed in this service with his usual vigour. He issued repeated Proclamations . . . and he volunteered to act as a mediator between the insurgents and the Emperor.' By Cochrane's own account, 'Had the Pernambucans been aware of the want of concord between the Emperor's intentions and those of his ministers, who had forced themselves upon him – the probability is that they would have supported, instead of denouncing his government'. However, persuasion could no more budge Carvalho than threats of blockade or bombardment; and at this juncture Maria Graham, who knew the rebel leader personally, arrived unexpectedly on the packet from Falmouth and offered to act as go-between.

Over fruit and wine she first tried to arrange a meeting with Cochrane on board a French brig of war, and when Carvalho declined, delivered Cochrane's terms, which provided for the safe conduct abroad of the rebel leaders and their families. Carvalho countered by pointing out that 'Your not having been rewarded for the first expedition affords a justifiable inference that you will get nothing for the second.' This shaft must have gone home, but when he went on to offer Cochrane 400,000 *milreis* to change sides, he was met with an outraged refusal.

Since the Roads of Pernambuco were too shallow to allow the *Pedro Primeiro* to stand inshore, the schooner *Leopoldina* was fitted out with mortars and threw a few shells into the city, but without much effect. A sudden storm now set in, setting the *Pedro Primeiro* adrift through the loss of her anchors, and Cochrane, whose heart was evidently not in the affair, seized this as a pretext for retiring to Bahia. The city of Pernambuco was in fact taken shortly afterwards by the troops under General Lima.

Carvalho managed to escape on a fishing boat and found sanctuary on the British corvette *Tweed*. Although he took no further part in the rebellion his project for a 'Confederation of the Equator' had kindled a spark in the provinces of Paraíba, Río Grande do Norte and Ceará. Cochrane was later to write that 'I could not but see that, in the outset of the revolt, both insurgents and leaders had good cause to be dissatisfied with the central government at Rio de Janeiro'. Nevertheless, true to his instructions, he stamped out the rebellion, finally dropping anchor at Maranham.

Here he found his marquisate in renewed chaos, with the army in revolt against the President, Miguel Bruce, a Brazilian of Scottish ancestry. Both parties claimed that they were supporting Dom Pedro, while accusing their opponents of plotting to form a republic;

and Cochrane's advent was received with relief by the inhabitants and also by the British and French consuls, who begged him to restore order. When it transpired that Bruce had enlisted a private negro army and was terrorising the city, Cochrane had him arrested, meanwhile replacing him by his own nomineee, Manuel Telles de Silva Loba, on whom he could rely in implementing a typically forthright scheme for recouping himself and the squadron.

It was now New Year, 1825. 'Worn down in health,' writes Cochrane, 'by the harassing duties of the naval, military, and civil departments, the conduct of all these wholly devolving upon me, whilst the Ministry at Rio, by withholding instructions, neither incurred trouble nor responsibility . . . I was heartily sick of the ingratitude and misrepresentation with which the service of having twice secured the northern provinces to Brazil was met on the part of the Administration . . .'

On New Year's Day he again wrote to Dom Pedro offering his resignation and next drew up a detailed statement of Portuguese property captured by the squadron at Maranham the year before, which he forwarded to the provincial government with a demand for payment, at the same time indicating that he was prepared to take one quarter (or approximately £25,000) of the total of 424,196,461 *reis* in settlement.

'In doing this,' as Armitage drily notes, 'he had nothing to apprehend from the President. This individual, the humble ex-secretary to the provincial Government, owed his elevation solely to the favour of his Lordship; the besieging army had been dispersed, and the troops of Bruce were prisoners.' The treasury at first refused, but to quote Armitage again, 'His Lordship, in consequence, appeared in person . . . and proceeded to urge the claims of his squadron with great firmness. From a glance at the respective position of the parties, it is easy to perceive how the dispute must necessarily terminate. A unanimous vote was finally passed, that as the Treasury was nearly empty, the Custom-house should furnish the stipulated sum . . .'

It was an arrangement in fact which cost the local authorities nothing, since the monies would otherwise have been forwarded to Rio, but it is hardly surprising that, as Cochrane was later to write, 'No small amount of obloquy has been attached to me with regard to this act of justice, the only one the squadron was every likely to obtain'. He was roundly denounced as 'a pirate and robber' by sections of the local press, but nevertheless remained calmly at anchor off Maranham while the monies came slowly in. When a new governor arrived from Rio and attempted to intervene with a show of force, he was promptly arrested and despatched in a brig of war to Pará 'to await the determination of the Emperor'. Cochrane undoubtedly felt that right was on his side; he was prepared to brook no interference; and payment of the 106,000 *milreis* was finally completed in May.

Cochrane had received no reply to four requests to resign his command. He had no further wish 'to do dirty work for a worthless administration, least of all in a latitude 3° south of the Equator'; he foresaw that a prompt return to Rio would involve him in endless altercation; and 'resolved upon a short run into a more bracing Northerly atmosphere, which would answer the double purpose of restoring our health, and of giving us clear offing for our subsequent voyage to Rio de Janeiro'.

Having distributed the prize money, he therefore placed Captain Jowett in command of the *Pedro Primeiro* with instructions to proceed to Rio and himself sailed north in the *Piranga*. The frigate sprang her main topmast during a storm off the Azores, and it was then discovered that the salt provisions were bad, 'mercantile ingenuity having resorted to the device of placing good meat at the top and bottom of the barrel; whilst the middle, being composed of unsound provisions, had tainted the whole'. Whether or not it had been his intention to sail for England in the first place, he now called a meeting of the ship's officers, and in view of the unfriendly reception to be expected in Portugal, France or Spain, it was decided to make for Portsmouth. Here, too, there were dangers in arriving in the warship of an unrecognized foreign state in the teeth of the Foreign Enlistment Act, and on reaching Spithead on 24 June, 1825, he was careful to enquire of the Port Admiral whether the *Piranga*'s salute would be returned. To his great relief the Admiral did him full honours, 'thus, for the first time, was the flag of his Imperial Majesty saluted by an European state, and the independence of Brazil virtually acknowledged'.

The quarrel with the Brazilian government, rankling over the seizure of prize money and the departure of the *Piranga* for England without orders, rumbled on for months; and Cochrane was soon involved in acrimonious exchanges with the Brazilian envoy in London.

It would be tedious to enter into the details of the dispute, set out at interminable length in the pages of his *Narrative of Services*. For the remainder of his long life Cochrane was preoccupied with obtaining what he regarded as his fair dues from the governments of Chile and Brazil. After years of correspondence, the Chilean government awarded him £6000 in 1845 and (at the advanced age of eighty) admiral's pay for life. Thirty years after he had left the service of Brazil, he was awarded half of the *interest* on the sum at issue, although one Commissioner was of opinion that it was 'little conformable to the dignity of Brazil, to enter at this distance in time, into questions of money with one to whom they owed so much'. Another stated forthrightly that 'as a commemoration of the benefits which Brazil had derived from Lord Cochrane, there was no other conclusion but that he ought to be paid the whole sum which he claimed'. After his death in 1860 a more generous administration paid his family £40,000 of the £100,000 he had claimed, but his services were more fittingly commemorated in 1902, when in the presence of a guard of honour from the warship *Floriano*, the Brazilian Ambassador placed a wreath on his tomb in Westminster Abbey, paying tribute to him as the 'South American Lafayette'.

Cochrane's naval career did not end in Brazil. He later achieved his ambition of leading an expedition to Greece, though with less spectacular results than in Chile, Peru or Brazil. He was finally reinstated as an admiral in the Royal Navy, and when war broke out between Britain and Russia in 1853 was seriously considered for the command in the Baltic at the advanced age of seventy-nine. The First Lord of Admiralty wrote to Queen Victoria at the time: 'his energies and faculties are unbroken, and with his accustomed courage he volunteers for the service, yet on the whole there is reason to apprehend that he might deeply commit the force under his command in some desperate enterprise, where the chance of success would not counteract the risk of failure and of the fatal consequences which might ensue. Age has not abated the adventurous spirit of this gallant officer, which no authority could restrain...'

For all his emphasis on the monetary value of his services and his shortcomings as a politician, in the military sphere Thomas Cochrane contributed as much to the liberation of South America as any other single man, with the exception of Bolívar and San Martín. *The Times* was only being just when it wrote of him in its obituary:

> There have been greater heroes, because there have been heroes with greater opportunities; but no soldier or sailor of modern times ever displayed a more extraordinary capacity than the man who now lies dead. He not only never knew fear, but he never knew perplexity . . .

VIII WAR IN The RIVER PLATE

WHEN Cochrane returned to England in 1825, Dom Pedro was embroiled in hostilities not only in the north of Brazil, but in the Banda Oriental (see Chapters I and II) to the south. Although Cochrane does not say as much in his *Narrative of Services*, it was perhaps the conviction that he might soon find himself ordered to attack the patriots of the Banda Oriental, a cause for which he could have had even less enthusiasm than the suppression of rebels in Pernambuco, that motivated his abrupt departure from Brazil. Certain it is that most of his ships and their crews under his former officers, such as Grenfell, Shepherd and Beaurepaire, played a leading part in the naval battles of the war with the United Provinces of Buenos Aires, which broke out in October 1825.

There had been drastic changes in the Banda Oriental since General Alvear's *porteño* army, with Admiral Brown's support, had captured Montevideo from the Spaniards in 1814 on behalf of the United Provinces; and it was subsequently lost to the Uruguayan patriot, Artigas. On the somewhat specious grounds that Artigas was a dangerous revolutionary and an undesirable neighbour and that Buenos Aires had been unable to bring him to book, a Portuguese fleet and army were despatched to the Plate in June 1816 with the ostensible object of recovering the territory for Ferdinand VII of Spain. In January 1817 General Lecor entered Montevideo, proclaimed himself Captain-General of the province and, with the help of Portuguese troops released from the battlefields of Europe, defeated the *gauchos* under Artigas, who then fled to Paraguay. Portugal had thus achieved her age-long ambition of controlling the all-important north bank of the River Plate, but at the expense of heated protests from Spain and Buenos Aires and a diplomatic furore in the capitals of Europe. The Portuguese nevertheless rode out the storm, and in July 1821 Lecor convened a congress in Montevideo, which voted in favour of federation with Portugal.

When Brazilian independence was declared in 1822, the garrison of Montevideo held out for a year on behalf of metropolitan Portugal, and it was only after the city had been retaken by General Lecor that its *Cabildo* (or city council) adhered to the new constitution and the province was unceremoniously transferred from one foreign power to another. Nevertheless, the *Diario Fluminense* of Rio de Janeiro

123

was soon to report in glowing terms of a portrait of Dom Pedro presented to the chamber:

' "Who is this," exclaimed the worthy members of the Cabildo, in this overflowing ebullience of loyalty: "who is this that approaches majestically, with an august yet juvenile, sweet and affable aspect, with a gallant and heroic air, and to whom our tribute of affection is rendered between perturbation and pleasure, as though we were in the presence of an angel of the Lord?" There can be no doubt it is Pedro the First! . . . It is a fact, Sire, your Monte Video loves you, and can say to you as a bride, I am my lover's, and my lover is mine!'

Needless to say, the sentiments of the comfortable merchants in Montevideo and La Colonia found no echo in Buenos Aires or among the turbulent and freedom-loving *gauchos*, who had supported Artigas and still ranged the vast, undulating plains of the interior at will. Meanwhile, Sucre's victory at Ayacucho had encouraged a small group of Uruguayan patriots to form a secret society in Buenos Aires, the *Caballeros Orientales*; and, while not as yet giving direct aid to the patriots across the river, the government of the United Provinces made no attempt to disguise its sympathies or to prevent open appeals for weapons and ammunition.

On a dark and stormy night in April 1825, the famous Thirty-three, headed by the exiled Colonel Juan Antonio Lavalleja, crossed the River Plate in an open boat and landed unopposed. The *gauchos* flocked in from all sides, and in Armitage's words, 'there now commenced a guerrilla war, in which the skirmishes in every instance terminated in favour of the Gauchos . . . When least expected, they would sweep like a whirlwind round the outskirts of the Brazilian army; throw down the horses with their bolas*; entangle the riders in their lassos; and, after depriving the unfortunate wretches of life, again instantaneously disappear.'

By September, the original thirty-three had so grown in numbers

---

* Armitage describes the *bolas* as 'Three heavy spherical stone balls, each enclosed in a casing of tanned hide and attached to thongs about four feet in length, which are again attached to each other at the opposite extremities. When thrown, the Gaucho seizes one of these balls, and whirls the other two over his head, until they separate, after the manner of the governing balls of a steam engine. When stretched to their full extent, they are flung so, that the central point, where the thongs are attached, falls full upon the object aimed at; and the balls are then coiled round and round with irresistible violence.'

that, well-supplied with arms from Buenos Aires, Lavelleja was able to inflict a decisive defeat at Sarandí on 2200 Portuguese troops of the line. Although Lecor remained in firm possession of the large cities of Montevideo and La Colonia, his troops 'were unable to venture outside the walls without danger of being cut off by their opponents; and on one occasion it is recorded, that the sentinel on guard at the gates of Monte Video was actually *lassoed*, and carried off by a Gaucho'.

Outright hostilities between Brazil and the United Provinces broke out when, in the wake of the Battle of Sarandí, the Buenos Aires Congress formally incorporated the Banda Oriental into the United Provinces. This was considered an act of war by Brazil; and a squadron of thirty sail under Admiral Lôbo was despatched to the Plate to enforce a blockade of Buenos Aires, effective from 21 December, 1825.

The ensuing war was in fact largely fought at sea by ships very largely manned by British and other foreign sailors. It has been estimated that there were no less than 1200 English seamen in the Brazilian navy alone; most of the commanders on both sides were English, and the constant desertions from British merchantmen arriving in Rio de Janeiro was a cause of acute concern to the commanders of the Navy's South American station.

Strangely enough, the command of the United Provinces' naval squadron was not in the first place offered to Admiral Brown (see pages 30 to 39), but to Captain Robert Ramsay of the Royal Navy. Ramsay had earlier won the trust and respect of the Buenos Aireans by his conduct during the Spanish blockade of 1810, when, on threat of being blown out of the water in his little schooner H.M.S. *Mistletoe* by the Spanish Admiral, he had insisted upon the release of two English brigs and then escorted them into Buenos Aires. Having signed an agreement with the Ministry of Marine in November 1825, he chivalrously declined the appointment of commander-in-chief in favour of the well-tried Brown, offering him his own sword – which was used by Brown during the war and is now in the National Historical Museum in Buenos Aires. Ramsay nevertheless acted as London agent for the United Provinces, and though his plans for purchasing and arming a large East Indiaman came to nothing through lack of funds, he was instrumental in recruiting some experienced British naval officers for the squadron.

It was therefore Brown who resumed command; and at the same time the government issued letters of marque, authorizing privateers to seize Brazilian ships and property.

In the absence of a regular navy, privateers sailing under Argentine colours had earlier played an important part in harassing Spanish shipping during the period 1814–20, and many of the *armadores*, who bore the cost of fitting out the ships, and most of their commanders were British or North American. One of the most famous of such expeditions, that of Admiral Brown to the Pacific and Guayaquil has already been described (pages 34–38).

After parting company with Brown in the Galapagos Islands, his companion in arms, Captain Bouchard, returned to Buenos Aires and embarked in his prize, the *Consecuencia*, renamed *La Argentina*, on an even more extensive privateering cruise, which spanned the globe. Setting sail for the Philippines by way of the Cape of Good Hope, Madagascar and Malaya, he next crossed the Pacific via the Sandwich Islands, finally preying on shipping along the coasts of California and South America. An early opponent of slavery, slavers of any nationality were as much his target as Spanish merchantmen. His adventurous career was finally brought to an end when, justifiably or not, he was arrested as a pirate by Admiral Cochrane off Valparaiso.

Another famous privateer of the period was an American from a well-known Baltimore family, James Chayter, who first arrived in the Plate in 1816 with a cargo of arms for the Republic. He was subsequently given the rank of Lieutenant-Colonel of Marine and, with his corvette *Independencia del Sur*, made a number of daring descents on the coast of the Spanish mainland, lurking off Cadiz, capturing numerous merchantmen and escorting them across the Atlantic to Buenos Aires.

For all this activity, the government in Buenos Aires found itself gravely short of ships and sailors when war broke out in 1825. All that it could put at Brown's disposal were the brigs *General Balcarce* and *General Belgrano*, armed with fourteen and sixteen cannon respectively, a few small gunboats, and two other small craft mounting a gun on the poop. It was with these slender resources that he faced a Brazilian navy of some eighty ships, among them Cochrane's former flagship, the seventy-four, *Pedro Primeiro*, nine or ten frigates, and numerous corvettes, brigs and schooners.

The saving grace was that the anchorage at Buenos Aires consisted of a shallow inner roadstead divided from the deep-water outer roads by a sandbank reaching some five miles out into the wide

Plate estuary, through which the connecting channel was narrow and circuitous. The inner roadstead was completely inaccessible to the heavy Brazilian ships, while Brown's shallow-drafted vessels could come and go at will, sheltering when necessary under the shore batteries.

The first brush with the blockading squadron took place on 12 January, 1826, when Brown sallied out, cut off a Brazilian gunboat and towed it back into port in full sight of the cheering citizens, watching from their housetops. The government now took steps to reinforce his little flotilla by buying and fitting out a number of small merchantmen, of which the largest was the 350-ton *Comercio de Lima*, renamed the *25 de Mayo* in commemoration of the revolution of that date. It also despatched an envoy to the friendly government of Chile to buy three of the ships from Cochrane's former squadron, now laid up after the successful termination of hostilities with Spain: The *O'Higgins*, *Independencia* and *Chacabuco*. The squadron left Valparaiso on 26 May; but the *O'Higgins*, which had seen such signal service at Valdivia and elsewhere, foundered in mountainous seas off Cape Horn with the loss of its captain and all five hundred hands; the *Independencia* ran aground and was sold for firewood; and only the *Chacabuco* reached Buenos Aires in safety. The new ships were crewed with English and North American sailors and a polyglot mixture of immigrants and country people from the interior without experience of the sea.

Meanwhile, Brown, in his new flagship, the *25 de Mayo*, made a further foray against the much superior Brazilian fleet on 9 February. Deserted by the other ships of his squadron – whose commanders were later suspended – Brown fought it out alone for an hour, subsequently renewing the action to rescue his gunboats and forcing the Brazilians to retire.

His next venture was a bold attempt on the strongly fortified port of La Colonia del Sacramento across the River Plate. Here, he overreached himself, since the only real hope of success lay in a simultaneous attack by the land forces of Colonel Lavalleja, which failed to materialize. Nevertheless, appearing in force on 25 February, in the manner of Cochrane he at once despatched a message to the Governor, calling upon him to surrender in the name of humanity. But Brigadier Manuel Jorge Rodrigues was of sterner stuff than his compatriots in the north and at once replied that the issue must be decided by force of arms. In a brisk exchange of fire with the forts, the *General Belgrano* ran aground and was destroyed. Nothing daunted, Brown withdrew his ships out of range of the forts and, pending the arrival of a detachment of six gunboats from Buenos Aires, reiterated his demand for surrender. This was met by the terse reply from Rodrigues: 'Tell the General that I have said what I have said.'

On the night of the 27th, the gunboats were sent in with instructions to capture three small warships lying in the harbour. The brig *Real Pedro* was stormed and burnt, but an attempted landing was disastrously repulsed with the destruction of two of the gunboats and the capture of three others. In all, the Argentinians lost some 200 men; in the meantime a Brazilian schooner had slipped out of port to summon aid from Admiral Lôbo, and Brown withdrew to Buenos Aires on 13 March.

From this point the tactics of the rival squadrons have been well-described by Prado Maia in *A Marinha de guerra do Brazil*: 'The bravery of the Argentine commander-in-chief cannot be denied. Either from a genuine wish to fight a superior force, as was ours, or with the simple intention of demonstrating the activity of his squadron and justifying additions to it, Brown regularly abandoned the safe harbourage of Buenos Aires and came out to face the cannon of the Brazilian fleet . . . Each commander was eager to fight, but under the conditions most favourable to him. Thus, whenever the ships were engaged, the Brazilian admiral tried to lure the Argentine away from port, where his own could manoeuvre without danger of running aground. The Argentinean commander, on the other hand, because his ships were of shallow draught, attempted to draw our ships towards shoals or narrow and winding channels, so that these became a new enemy for an incautious adversary. Most of these encounters, therefore, almost always developed in the same way. On seeing the hostile ships leave port, the Brazilian warships stood out to sea, leaving the enemy to follow. When it was judged that there was sufficient room for manoeuvre, they put about and gave chase. The tactics of the *porteños* were the exact reverse. They would follow the Brazilian squadron to a certain point, and when it put about and the first shots were exchanged, Brown's ships promptly headed for port, hoping that in the heat of the chase, our vessels would run aground on some hidden sandbank . . .'

Two such encounters developed into a personal duel between Brown and Captain (later Vice-Admiral) James Norton, perhaps his most formidable adversary during the war. Born in London in 1789, Norton entered the Brazilian service in 1823, first commanding the frigate *Piranya*, before transferring to the *Nitheroy* after its epic

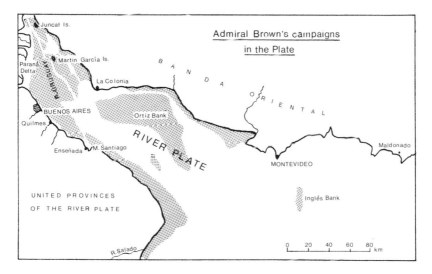

Admiral Brown's campaigns in the Plate

pursuit of the Portuguese fleet to the Tagus. The two first exchanged broadsides when the *Nitheroy* beat off an attack on Montevideo on 11 April, 1826. Returning to the fray, Brown made a second surprise attack by night on the 27. Argentinian and Brazilian accounts of this engagement somewhat differ, but what is clear is that Brown was doubly mistaken, first in taking the frigate *Imperatriz* for the *Nitheroy*, and then in hailing her in English under the impression that she might, after all be a British ship of war. By answering back in English, the Brazilian vessel gained time to organize her defences, and though a resolute attempt was subsequently made to board her, it was beaten off with heavy loss on both sides.

It was not long before the Brazilians retaliated by appearing in force off Buenos Aires, and Brown sallied out to fight. Both his flagship, the *25 de Mayo*, and the *Nitheroy* ran aground on the Ortiz bank and fought it out, broadside to broadside, after the other ships of their squadrons had abandoned them. Once again this encounter ended in stalemate; both combatants eventually floated off, Brown returning to Buenos Aires, and Norton to Montevideo.

In spite of the great discrepancy between the size and armament of the squadrons, Admiral Lôbo had proved singularly ineffective either in enforcing a complete blockade or in preventing raids on the Brazilian coast by Argentine privateers, while Brown emerged from Buenos Aires more or less at will to carry out destructive raids on Brazilian shipping and strong points, such as La Colonia. A further cause of irritation in Rio de Janeiro was the abandonment of

129

the strategic island of Martín García in the mouth of the Uruguay River, with results that were shortly to prove disastrous. Lôbo was therefore replaced by Vice-Admiral Rodrigo Pinto Guedes, who arrived in Montevideo on 12 May, 1826, and reorganized the Brazilian fleet as four divisions: the first was charged with long range operations; the second, under Norton, with the blockade of Buenos Aires; the third with the policing of the Uruguay and Paraná rivers; while the fourth was held in reserve.

The first fruit of his command was the severe reverse inflicted on Brown at Quilmes on 11 June. Challenged by Norton off Buenos Aires, Brown emerged in force with orders to his commanders to go down fighting rather than strike their colours. The two squadrons manoeuvred in parallel line of battle, then Brown, vastly outnumbered by twenty-two ships, 300 cannon and 2000 men to the eight ships, 109 cannon and 800 men of his own flotilla, ordered his ships to cut the enemy line and advanced to the attack in the *25 de Mayo*. He was not supported by the rest of his squadron, which was soon in full retreat to Buenos Aires, and the flagship came under destructive fire from the Brazilian ships, which closed in on all sides. Holed in some thirty places, it ran aground, and such was the carnage aboard that Brown, himself injured by a ricocheting cannon ball, ordered his men below to avoid further casualties. At this juncture the Argentinean squadron ventured out to his aid, and transferring his flag to the *República*, he was able to make his escape. The *25 de Mayo*, reduced to a floating shambles, was towed into port, but was beyond repair. On the Brazilian side, Captain Grenfell, who had led the attack in the *Caboclo*, was severely wounded and lost his right arm.

Brown was not the man to be discouraged by this mauling and shortly afterwards, running the gauntlet of the blockade, made junction with the *Chacabuco*, newly arrived from Chile under the command of Captain George Binnon, and carried the war into the enemy's camp by declaring a 'blockade' of Rio de Janeiro. Between them the two ships captured some fifteen merchantmen laden with sugar, coffee and other commodities and attacked a number of offshore islands. The object of the expedition was, however, psychological; and in this it succeeded by frightening off neutral shipping, causing alarm in Rio and outspoken criticism of the Brazilian naval commanders in the Plate, and the diversion of a squadron of fourteen ships under Norton, in the belief that the whole Argentinian squadron was involved.

Much more important in military terms was Brown's expedition to the Uruguay River in January 1827. News had reached Buenos Aires of the despatch by Admiral Pinto Guedes of a powerful flotilla to the Uruguay, so as to impede the operations of the Argentinean land forces under General Alvear. The seventeen ships under Captain Jacinto de Senna Pereyra, the so-called *3° Division bloqueadora*, had been carefully chosen for their shallow draught and assembled over a period of some months.

Brown immediately issued an order of the day: 'Glory beckons, and our small squadron will gain new laurels on this occasion. The commanders of all our ships of war are invited to accompany me on a short but honourable cruise.' The cruise was to prove anything but short, and its outcome was Brown's most resounding victory.

Entering the Uruguay River on 28 December, he proceeded upstream and found Pereyra's ships at anchor off the mouth of the Río Negro in an inaccessible position defended by a sand bar. When Captain Coe, whom he despatched under a flag of truce to demand the surrender of the enemy squadron, was treacherously imprisoned, he retaliated with a brisk cannonade and then fell back down the river, installing a battery at Punta Gordon to command the narrows at this point, so bottling up the *3° Division* in the upper waters of the Uruguay. He next decided to fortify the Island of Martín García, further south and recently abandoned by the Brazilians, as a more permanent base, and leaving his squadron on guard, sailed back to Buenos Aires in the *Sarandí* to obtain artillery and reinforcements.

Meanwhile, Pinto Guedes decided to reinforce Captain Pereyra and despatched a further 'Auxiliary Division' of nine ships under Captain Federico Mariath. When Brown returned in the *Sarandí* early in January, it was therefore to find that the main channel to the south of Martín García was blockaded by Mariath's ships and that his own squadron was trapped between the two Brazilian forces. Taking to a whaleboat, Brown nevertheless made his way back to Martín García by one of the tortuous channels of the Paraná delta, meanwhile instructing Lieutenant-Colonel Espora to return to Buenos Aires, lighten the *Sarandí* and follow him – a manoeuvre which was successfully accomplished.

Mariath's orders were to liaise with Pereyra and to take the Argentinean squadron from the rear; but fortification of Martín García had been proceeding apace, and although the island was grossly under-garrisoned, a half-hearted attempt to storm it and make junction with the *3° Division* was easily beaten off, and when Brown decided to give battle to Pereyra, Mariath made no attempt to intervene. The two squadrons came face to face on 8 February, 1827, upstream of Martín García and opposite the small island of Juncal; but contrary winds prevented them from getting to grips. During the ensuing night Brown made his usual meticulous preparations and fell upon the *3° Division* at dawn next morning before the ships were fully ready for combat, causing instant confusion and havoc. Pereyra, with three of his ships, was captured; a hospital ship was taken later in the day; others were burnt by their crews; and of those which took flight up the river, only two escaped. Mariath's squadron, which had looked impotently on, now sheered off and found refuge at La Colonia.

Apart from its great moral impact, the victory of Juncal had important strategic results. Although the *3° Division* was only a small part of the Brazilian fleet, it embraced most of the vessels of shallow draft capable of navigating the Uruguay; and the river thereafter became the preserve of the Buenos Aireans. Communication with Alvear's army in the Banda Oriental were now assured, while the fortified island of Martín García served as a haven for neutral merchantmen or coastal shipping running the Brazilian blockade.

Brown was not to repeat this success, and indeed his little squadron was more or less annihilated in an action fought off Monte Santiago in the Plate estuary in April 1827. Earlier that year the Brazilians had sent a flotilla of four ships under Captain James Shepherd (who had earlier taken over command of the *Piranga* from Admiral Cochrane on his arrival in England) to the Río Negro in Patagonia, an anchorage used by the Argentinean privateers for the safe-keeping of their prizes and repair of their ships. It had ended in disaster, when one of the Brazilian ships was wrecked and the other three captured, during a foray ashore in which Shepherd was killed and his men overpowered.

It was Brown's intention to proceed to Patagonia and to incorporate the three captured ships in his own squadron, so strengthening it for raids on Brazilian commerce. Shortly after leaving Buenos Aires, he was, however, intercepted by Norton's squadron of sixteen sail on the morning of 7 April. In making for the shelter of Ensenada, two of the Argentinean ships, the *Independencia* and *República*, ran aground and came under heavy fire. Desperate efforts were made to float them off during the night, but to no avail. The action was resumed next day, when the *Independencia*, after expending all her 3000 rounds of ammunition and suffering 200 direct hits, struck colours. Her crew was transferred to the *Sarandí* and she was subsequently boarded and burnt by the Brazilians. The *República* was also abandoned and set alight by her own crew, and at the end of the day the *Sarandí* and *Congreso* made good their escape to Buenos Aires with the survivors. Captain Drummond of the *Independencia* was killed; Grenville, in command of the *República*, lost an arm; while Brown himself was wounded. In all, the Argentinians suffered 160 casualties, including fifty-five dead, a crippling blow for a squadron whose complement numbered only 400 men.

The Battle of Monte Santiago effectively put an end to large-scale naval operations on the part of the Argentinians, who henceforth intensified the attacks of their privateers, to the severe detriment of Brazilian trade and commerce. As in the days of the war with Spain, some of these corsairs were fitted out by private *armadores*, but the most effective operated within the national squadron under the command of such aggressive seamen as De Kay, Fournier, Fourmartín, Allen, King, Coe, Binnon and Masson. An idea of the scale of this war of attrition and the fortunes of its progatonists can be gained from the Brazilian naval records, which lists scores of major encounters between June 1827 and August 1828, when hostilities ended. The following are typical:

25 June. 1827 – The frigate *Príncipe Imperial*, repels an attack by the corsair *General Brandzen*. This corsair, commanded by the Englishman George de Kay, was armed with 4 carronades of calibre 8, two of 12 and twelve cannon of 12. Its crew was North American and English.

26 June, 1827 – The same corsair, *General Brandzen*, captures the schooner *Isabel Maria* of the Imperial squadron after gallant resistance.

11 September, 1827 – The Brazilian brig *Cacique* (commander George Manson) is taken off the coast of Pernambuco by the corsair *General Brandzen*.

28 September, 1827 – The brig *Imperial Pedro* (commander Joaquim Leal Ferreira) captures the corsair *Patagonés* (commander George Lewis Love). Shortly before, this corsair had taken the Brazilian transport *Pojuca*, commanded by Captain José Lourenço da Silva.

25 January, 1828 – The corvette *Maria Isabel* (commander Feliciano Inácio Maia), conveying 12 merchantmen from Santos to Rio de Janeiro, is attacked by the Argentinean corsair *Niger* (commander John Coe) and engaged in violent combat. Boarded three times, the

corvette in the end repelled its attacker, which suffered much damage and the loss of 50 men.

27 January, 1828 – Pursued by the brigs *Maranhão*, *Caboclo*, *Pirajá* and the schooner *Constança*, the corsairs *El-Bravo* and *Federal-Argentino* run aground off the coast of Barregā and are burnt.

31 January, 1828 – Nine leagues from the Island of Rasa, the corsair *Niger* captures the packet *Sete de Janeiro*.

23 March, 1828 – The brig *Caboclo* (Captain James Inglis) pursues, attacks and captures, with all her crew, the corsair *Niger* (commander John Coe).

16 June, 1828 – The Brazilian ships under the command of Captain James Norton give chase to the corsair *General Brandzen*, which ran aground while seeking shelter at Fort Punta Lara. It was strongly attacked and finally burnt. In this combat Norton lost his right arm.

30 August, 1828 – Pursuit and destruction of the two merchantmen *Hussar* and *Lord Eldon*. These two ships, under the protection of the corsair *Empresa* and an Argentinean gunboat, were trying to run the blockade. Attacked by the brig *Caboclo* and the schooner *Dois de Julio* and bombarded by the gunboat *19 de Outubro*, they ran aground under the battery of Salado, where they were boarded and burnt by our men. At the same time there was a brisk exchange of fire with the battery and the corsair.

In his *Vida de Brown*, the Argentinean naval historian, Héctor Ratto, states that some three hundred prizes were taken by the privateers during the first eighteen months of their operations, and 145 in the subsequent eleven before hostilities ended. Whatever the tally in terms of captured ships and encounters at sea, the outcome in terms of trade and finance was enormously in favour of the United Provinces.

Thus, the English newspaper in Buenos Aires, *The British Packet*, wrote in May 1827 that 'The damage inflicted is immense. Many of the corsairs, and probably all, have made successful voyages to the coasts of Brazil and, if the war continues, the commerce of that country will be shaken to its foundations. It is useless to talk of convoys; even if the Brazilian navy had five times as many ships as it has, it could not give adequate protection to its commerce.' This is borne out by an article dated 8 August, 1828, in the *Aurora Fluminense* of Rio de Janeiro, which spoke of 'the national losses resulting from the destruction, particularly in Rio Grande; the loss of commerce, the stagnation of agriculture and manufacture' and gloomily fixed the indemnity for 'the imprudent seizure' of foreign merchantmen in the Plate at 25 million pesos, on top of an annual expenditure of 14 million pesos on the army and navy.

In drawing up a balance sheet, Ratto estimates that the military expenditure of the United Provinces was only one quarter that of Brazil and notes that the newspapers of the period speak of an abundance of imported commodities in Buenos Aires, thanks to the operations of the corsairs. As regards the effect of the war on the Republic, his considered opinion is that 'If one takes note that the number of [foreign] ships docking at the port [of Buenos Aires] in the five years preceding the war was 256 and in the five years following it, 200; that during the war many ships berthed at other ports on the river; and above all that the 445 prizes are equivalent to an annual arrival of 148 ships, one is driven to the conclusion that the volume of Argentinean commerce cannot have been affected by more than 30 per cent – in spite of the disproportion of naval forces, which should totally have eliminated it.'

Brazil had been no more successful on land than at sea. The war was unpopular in Rio, and a perennial problem was the enlistment of native troops. As Armitage reports, 'Notwithstanding their abhorrence of military life, they were seized like malefactors, and after being bound and crammed into the holds of filthy ships, were sent off to the bleak and dreary plains of the south', where they sickened and died in droves without meeting the enemy. The authorities then resorted to the engagement of Germans as colonists and their prompt drafting into the army. Even worse was the fate of three thousand Irish immigrants. 'From the landing place they were marched off to the barracks, in the Rua dos Barbonos, amid the taunts of the populace, and the jeers of multitudes of negroes, shouting and clapping their hands at the unexpected apparition of the "white slaves" . . . and the male portion of the colonists were clearly given to understand that they had no alternative, excepting either to enlist or starve.'

With material such as this, it is not surprising that Lecor should have had little success against the hard-bitten *gauchos* or the troops of General Alvear, dedicated to the cause of liberation. In an attempt to boost morale, Dom Pedro left for the battle front in person in 1826, but had got no farther than Rio Grande do Sul when he learned that his wife was mortally ill and hastily returned to the capital – but not before the ill-advised replacement of General Lecor by a court favourite, the Marquess of Barbecana, promptly routed at the Battle of Ituzaingó in February 1827.

It was becoming clear that neither side could hope for outright victory, and towards the end of 1827 the British government, concerned by the damage to the lucrative South American trade and further uneasy about the large-scale desertions from British ships and the wholesale involvement of its nationals in the war, threw its whole weight into achieving a settlement. In the opinion of the British Minister on the spot, the forceful Charles Gordon, it was a conflict 'than which none was ever waged more iniquitous or more disastrous to all parties concerned'.

He therefore proposed to the Brazilian government that the Banda Oriental should become a free and independent state through the mediation of the British government. His suggestion was agreed by both parties, but on his departure from Rio in August 1828, it was left to Lord Ponsonby to witness the signature of the preliminary convention of 27 August, 1828. In so doing he advised the agent from Buenos Aires that 'any retreat on his part from the engagements to me as a minister of the Mediating Sovereign, must originate the most serious question between His Majesty's government and the Argentine republic', at the same time repeating the threat 'in pretty strong terms' to the Brazilian minister. His plain speaking was hardly necessary: honour had been satisfied, and by now both sides were heartily tired of the war.

Of Brown's great personal contribution to the liberation of Uruguay – to which he further contributed by acting as one of the Argentine commissioners during the negotiations for the armistice – there can be no doubt. When his ship was in action he would regularly appear on deck in full dress uniform, with high boots, decorations and sword, making the rounds of the guns in full sight of the enemy and spurring their crews to greater efforts. A strict disciplinarian, a devout Catholic and frugal in his tastes – he drank nothing except a cup of tea and a glass of wine after lunch, and he had no use for coffee – he was nevertheless popular with his men, for whom he displayed a paternal concern. It is recorded that on one occasion, he appeared just as one of his sailors had had his leg amputated. In spite of the intense pain, the man broke out: '*Viva la Patria; viva Brown!*'

Ashore, his popularity knew no bounds; and he was the hero of Buenos Aires. After his encounter with Norton off Quilmes, he was welcomed by a delirious crowd, whole families driving down to the waterfront in their carriages and crowding out to the end of the mole, while Ratto writes of his reception after the victory of Juncal that: 'At dusk on February 10, 1827, Buenos Aires was vibrant with enthusiasm. There were bonfires, fireworks and bands paid for by public subscription, while the streets rang with cheers for the heroes of the navy and the army. One band, accompanied by an enthusiastic crowd singing the national anthem, went as far as the Quinta de Barracas [Brown's house]. All classes took part, the poor celebrating in the streets, and the rich holding parties until morning. One of the newspapers reported that no-one slept on that memorable night.'

A great lover of the theatre – on the back of one of the pages of his 'Diary of the Squadron's operations in the War against Brazil', he scribbled the beginnings of a play – he was fêted whenever he appeared at the theatre. His portrait was commissioned by public subscription and soon afterwards engraved by the French artist Douville, who writes of his lithograph: 'After we had engraved the portrait of Admiral Brown, on a small scale and very true to the original, and in spite of the price of two pesos, we were left without a single copy of the 2,000 we had pulled. During the printing our establishment was too small to keep pace with the demand, and the public was supplied by rota.'

After further services to the Republic, both in command of the squadron during a later conflict with Uruguay and as Governor Delegate of Buenos Aires, Brown died at midnight on 2 March, 1857, shortly beforehand turning to his friend, Colonel of Marine Alejandro Murature, and saying: 'I understand that we shall shortly be changing anchorage, since the pilot is now on board.' Next day the squadron which he had so long commanded paid its last respects by firing a salute every quarter-of-an-hour, and General Bartolomé Mitre echoed the feelings of every citizen of Brown's adopted country, when he said in his funeral oration: 'It would be impossible to recall all the famous adventures of Admiral Brown. We all remember how the thunder of his cannon in the waters of the Plate was the signal of victory and how at the sight of his masts Buenos Aires slept secure, while the Admiral kept guard on his poop.'

It is pleasant to record that in later years his old adversary Admiral Norton, also much honoured in the country of his adoption, Brazil, visited Brown to compare notes over the battles they had so heatedly contested. It seems that Norton said to him, 'If you had served the Empire instead of a Republic you would now be a Duke with a handsome pension' – to which Brown quietly replied: 'I know Buenos Aires will always remember my services.'

IX MERCHANT ADVENTURERS

THE Spanish embargo on foreign trade with her American colonies had first been breached when Sir Home Popham captured and briefly held Buenos Aires in 1806 (see page 18); and after Sir Samuel Auchmuty stormed Montevideo in the following year some six thousand British subjects are said to have entered the town, of whom two thousand were 'merchants, traders, adventurers'. Between 1808 and 1809 the Spanish merchant houses fought hard to retain their monopoly by raising loans and other means; but in issuing his *carta regia* of 1808, freeing Brazil from restrictions on trade with friendly nations, Dom John opened the floodgates for illegal imports into the Spanish colonies to the south.

'So great and unexpected was the influx of English manufactures into Rio de Janeiro,' writes a contemporary English traveller, John Mawe, 'that the rent of the houses to put them into became enormously dear. The bay was covered with ships, and the customhouse soon overflowed with goods: even salt, casks of ironmongery, and nails, salt-fish, hogsheads of cheese, hats, together with an immense quantity of crates and hogsheads of earthen and glass ware, cordage, bottled and barrelled porter, paints, gums, resin, tar, etc. were exposed, not only to the sun and rain, but to general depredation.'

As the Spaniards were driven from one after another of their former colonies, it seemed that El Dorado – of a sort – was now within reach of the bold merchant venturer, so that, speaking in a parliamentary debate in 1817, Lord Brougham could declare that 'There can be no field of enterprise so magnificent in promise, so well calculated to raise sanguine hopes, so congenial to the most generous sympathies, so consistent with the best and highest interests of England, as the vast continent of South America. He must indeed be more than temperate, he must be a cold reasoner, who can glance at those regions, and not grow warm.'

The early British traders were subjected to a bewildering variety of taxes, import duties and arbitrary exactions, and their fortunes waxed and waned with the ebb and flow of conquest – when an area was reoccupied by the Spaniards, as during Morillo's reoccupation of Venezuela and New Granada, they were, of course, promptly expropriated. To protect their interests, first on the Atlantic coast and later in Chile and Peru, the navy established a British South American station at Rio de Janeiro – in this instance it appears to have been a case of the Flag following Trade, rather than the other way round – and, as already noted (pages 27 and 29) its commodores acted as unofficial consuls and diplomats, while at the same time restricting the activities of privateers and conveying home vast quantities of specie on behalf of the traders.

Although many of the *entrepreneurs*, such as John Miers, the friend of Lord Cochrane and Maria Graham, who arrived in Chile with a shipload of machinery to set up a copper refinery, returned disillusioned and out of pocket, the rewards were sometimes enormous – thus, a consignment of salt bought for $200 in Buenos Aires and shipped to Paraguay by the Robertson brothers, fetched $4000 in Asunción – and attracted a band of adventurers as colourful as their compatriots in the armies and navies of the new republics.

There remain many questions to be answered – as to the risks run and the corresponding rewards; the extent to which British capital replaced Spanish; and the contribution of foreign loans and commercial activity to the eventual emergence of the new states – but perhaps the story of the Robertson brothers, John Parish and William, spanning Paraguay, the Argentine, Chile and Peru, is as illuminating as any.

That the three volumes of *Letters on Paraguay* were belatedly published in 1838–39 is a tribute to the Scots pertinacity of its authors, since in a last letter to the reader they describe how 'On one of those desperate nights of January last, when every inanimate substance in nature was congealed – when the roads were covered with snow, and the footpaths overlaid with slides – one of the authors of these *"Letters on Paraguay"* was travelling in that conveyance for all, an omnibus, from London to Kensington. He had his manuscript under his arm, having got it, after perusal, from the publisher. He got down from the omnibus; but in getting upon the footpath, he placed his foot on a slide, and came down upon the ice. He was stunned for a moment by the severity of the blow, and so acute, when he got up, was his pain, that he limped away from the scene of his calamity, without even a thought about the MS . . . Next morning handbills and newspapers proclaimed the loss, and offered the necessary reward; but never again did we set eyes upon our lost sheets . . .' And so, 'from the same original documents', the Robertsons doggedly set out 'to compile anew the seven hundred long pages which were irretrievably lost on a winter's night'.

John Parish Robertson first came to Buenos Aires with his father, a former Assistant Secretary to the Bank of Scotland, in 1807 in the wake of Popham's expedition. He returned in 1808, working as a clerk, until in December 1811, while still not twenty, he decided to explore the possibilites of trade with Paraguay. The former *Intendencia* had just cut loose both from Spain and the United Provinces and was soon to be dominated by the dictatorial and xenophobic Dr José Gaspar Rodriguez de Francia, who for most practical purposes isolated the country from the outside world until his death in 1840. After overcoming Francia's first suspicions, Robertson soon established a highly profitable business and was joined in 1814 by his younger brother, William.

He now proposed a visit to England and was summoned to the Consul's 'small and humble audience chamber', where he was immediately subjected to a long and impassioned harangue: '"Paraguay is in a more flourishing state now, than any of the countries around it; and while here all is order, subordination, and tranquillity, the moment you pass its boundary, the sound of cannon, and the din of discord salute your ears . . . The natives of Buenos Ayres are the most fickle, vain, volatile, and profligate of the whole of Spain's late dominions in this hemisphere; and therefore I am resolved to have nothing to do with the Porteños. My wish is to promote an intercourse with England . . ."'

'At this point of his oration the Consul rose with great emotion, but evident delight, from his chair, and calling to the sentinel at the door, desired him to order in the serjeant of the guard. On appearance of this person the Doctor gave him a significant and peremptory look, and told him emphatically to bring *"that"*. The serjeant withdrew, and in less than three minutes returned with four grenadiers at his back, bearing, to my astonishment, among them, a large hide package of tobacco of two hundred weight, a bale of Paraguay tea of similar dimensions and exterior, a demi-john of Paraguay spirits, a large loaf of sugar, and several bundles of cigars, tied and ornamented with variegated fillets. Last of all, came an old negress with some beautiful specimens of embroidered cloth made from Paraguay cotton, and used there by the luxurious as hand-towels and shaving cloths.'

Robertson was at first overwhelmed with this splendid parting gift, but much taken aback when he learned that he was expected to present himself at the House of Commons with the assorted merchandise and to offer a trade treaty and exchange of ambassadors with the Court of St. James's. Nevertheless, he decided that his only course 'was acquiescence; and to this I came, in spite of the strong sense of the ludicrous which arose upon my mind, as I drew a picture of myself forcing my way to the bar of the House of Commons; overpowering, with half-a-dozen porters, the Usher of the Black Rod; and delivering, in spite of remonstrance and resistance, at once my hide-bound bales of Paraguay merchandise, and the oration, verbatim, of the First Consul . . .

On his arrival in Buenos Aires, Robertson came to the conclusion that it was not worth his while to proceed to England with 'specimens of produce, which, if rejected by the House of Commons, and carried to the market, might have produced me twenty guineas'. He therefore decided to ship another cargo of goods to Paraguay, but in view of well-justified qualms about his reception by the disappointed Supremo, did his best to fulfil Francia's commissions and included in the shipment a variety of 'cocked hats, sashes, lace, musical instruments, military clothing, swords and pistols,' together with 'a few muskets and munitions of war'.

At this juncture he was asked by General Alvear to approach Francia with an offer of arms and ammunition in exchange for Paraguayan recruits to strengthen the army of the United Provinces. Unwilling to intervene in a potentially explosive political matter, he nevertheless agreed to deliver a sealed letter – later to cause him the loss of his concession in Paraguay.

Since the intervening territory was occupied by the troops of General Artigas (see page 31), now openly at war with the United Provinces, the only practicable route was by the River Paraná; and he duly set sail, armed with a licence from Captain Jocelyn Percy, commanding the British forces in the River Plate. Unfortunately, on going ashore one evening to shoot pheasant, he returned to find his vessel in possession of a band of cut-throat *gaucho* guerrillas and was promptly pinioned and tethered to a ring-bolt on deck. His assailants proceeded to break open the cases of wine and liquor and to ransack the ship. 'In exchange for my whole wardrobe, I had thrown over my shoulders a tattered great-coat, and tied around my waist a worn-out poncho. No shirt, no stockings, were allowed me . . . Many of the Artigueños, on the other hand, having put off similar garments, were now to be seen strutting about in Bond Street cut coats, leather breeches (they were the fashion in those days), Andre's hats, tight fits of boots, both top and Hessian, with broad-frilled shirts, and large ties of white cravat . . .'

Worse was to follow when he was twice taken ashore to face a firing squad, and he was saved only by a custom prevailing among the Artigueños 'that any soldier who had distinguished himself more, that is, had committed more daring excesses than another, was entitled to ask a favour ("pedir un favor", as they styled it) of his chief; and it was at the chief's peril that he refused to grant it. On the present occasion (and, to me, it was one of some emergency) an Indian stepped out of the ranks, and "asked his favour." That favour was not a light one in my eyes, for it was, that my life should be spared. "Que no se fusile," said the Indian, "let him not be shot."'

On being taken to the local headquarters at Bajada, Robertson had his second stroke of good fortune, being recognized on his way to jail by an old servant,who lost no time in riding to Buenos Aires with the news of his plight. 'No sooner had he delivered his plain, unvarnished tale, than every Englishman in the place (and Captain Percy at their head) was roused to indignation . . . A brig-of-war was instantly despatched to General Artigas' headquarters at Paysandú, with one of those peremptory communications from the British Officer in command which so often characterize our naval commanders . . .'

Delivered at Artigas' headquarters 'by a weather-beaten lieutenant, with a bold air and an uncompromising cocked-hat', Percy's letter produced immediate orders for Robertson's release and the restitution of his ship and property, 'but before these could reach Bajada, another messenger, sent by Captain Percy over-land, by way of Santa Fé, had penetrated to my lonely cell, and in company with the Governor, Hereñú, now rather trembling in his shoes, proclaimed to me that I was once more, – a free man.'

Robertson's first act on being released was to seek out the Indian to whom he owed his life and he found him 'squatted on the mud floor of his barracks, and engaged in play with his companions over a pack of cards . . . It was with some difficulty I could get the Indian for a moment to leave his squat position in the ring of gamblers; and when I asked him what had induced him to interfere on my behalf, his reply was, "Se me antojó no mas": that is, "the whim of the moment."' Robertson put a few gold guineas into his hand – to learn next day that they had instantly been gambled away.

Although the bulk of his property was duly restored, the uniforms and weapons so important to Francia were still missing, and Robertson next bearded 'the most excellent Protector of half the New World', whom he found 'seated on a bullock's skull, at a fire kindled on the mud floor of his hut, eating beef off a spit, and drinking gin out of a cow-horn!' He was courteously received by Artigas, who 'put into my hand his own knife, and a spit with a piece of beef beautifully roasted upon it', but as regards the missing muskets and apparel, the general could only offer his apologies: '"Look here," said he; and, so saying, he lifted up the lid of an old military chest, and pointed to a canvas bag at the bottom of it – "There," he continued, "is the whole stock of my cash; it amounts to 300 dollars; and where the next supply is to come from, I am as little aware as you are."'

Realising that it would be imprudent to press his claim, Robertson then waived it, but cannily obtained from Artigas 'as a token of his gratitude and good will, some important mercantile privileges connected with an establishment I had formed at Corrientes'. These were very shortly to prove the brothers' salvation, since far from sympathising with James Parish in his misadventure, Francia was doubly furious – both because an imperious letter to Artigas had failed to secure the release of his arms and because Robertson had been freed, not at his own insistence, but at that of Captain Percy. When William explained that the arms were considered as *matériel* of war and that the British commander could not therefore intervene, he burst out: '"When my interests are to be consulted, I am told that what is intended for my republic is to be left to the mercy of marauders and cut-throats, while British officers scandalously overlook my just claims on the gratitude of Great Britain! Know, then, that I will no longer permit you, or your brother, or any other British merchant to reside in my territory. If you cannot guarantee to me a free trade in arms, be assured that I will not concede to you a commerce in English *rags*."'

The final straw was the discovery next day that Artigas had recovered the sealed letter written by General Alvear and had had it printed. '"See," said he, "what your brother had had the insolence and hardihood to do! He has trafficked for arms against the blood of the Paraguayans! He has offered men for muskets! – he has dared to sell my people!"' When James Parish arrived in person shortly afterwards, his explanations were brushed aside and he was given forty-eight hours in which to leave the country, while William was grudgingly allowed two months to wind up their affairs.

Undismayed, the Robertsons now took full advantage of the concession granted them by Artigas in the Corrientes, the wide tract of cattle country lying between the Uruguay and Paraná rivers, desolated by the recent wars, but now returning to normality. Establishing two large collection centres, they organized wagon trains to collect the hides and hired a renowned Irish-born *gaucho* to protect their operation. The dried hides bought in Corrientes for 1½d a pound could be sold in Buenos Aires for 5½d and fetched 9d or 10d in Liverpool, while the hide of a horse bought for 3d could be sold in England for 7s or 8s. On the strength of these lucrative transactions, the Robertsons were able to withdraw from the rough and tumble and, at times, dangerous life in Corrientes.

The time was now ripe for John Parish to approach his millionaire grandfather, of the banking house of John Parish & Co, of Hamburg. Recently retired to Bath, the old man welcomed John as 'a chip of the old block' and enabled the brothers to set up their own houses in Liverpool and Buenos Aires; and they were soon the correspondents not only of the Parishes, but of the Barings and other banks, engaging in the import of such commodities as German linen from Hamburg and the export of Spanish dollars to India or jerked beef to Havana.

After San Martín's victories at Chacabuco and Maipú in 1817, Valparaiso rapidly became the most important port in the Pacific, and in the words of an English traveller, Samuel Haigh, its markets were 'quite glutted with every description of goods and wares'. The Robertsons were quick to move in, and in 1820 John Parish wound up his business in Liverpool, arriving in Santiago in April 1821 with the object of laying 'the foundation of prosperous and extensive establishments in Santiago'.

The magnet of the merchant adventurers was not, however, agricultural and poverty-stricken Chile, but Peru with its mineral deposits and mines; and the ships were lining up with their cargoes well ahead of San Martín's entry into Lima in July 1821. So Captain Basil Hall, of the British naval squadron, wrote of the opening of the port of Callao that its harbour was soon 'crowded with ships unloading rich cargoes; while the bay, to the distance of a mile from the harbour, was covered with others waiting for room to land their merchandise'.

It was not, however, until April 1822 that John Parish left Chile for Peru, where he stayed for fifteen months and with typical drive and business acumen was soon contracting for the supply of provisions to Callao. In a letter dated 11 June, 1823, his brother William, who had remained in Buenos Aires, refers to eight ships en route for Peru with goods to the value of $600,000, while General Miller refers to the 'great talent' with which he helped to equip an expedition against the royalists in the interior. In 1823 he was appointed commercial agent for the Peruvian government in London and played an important part in floating two loans on the booming London Capital market.

The Times of 14 October, 1822, reported of the rush to invest in the first of such loans that 'a scene of extreme confusion took place on the Royal Exchange, caused by the excessive competition to obtain shares'. The contractor, Thomas Kinder 'and his agents were forced by the multitude surrounding them from the Dutch walk, where the confusion began, to the opposite corner of the Exchange, where the Swedish merchants assemble. Here the brokers became so highly exasperated, being still unable to come to terms with the agents, that they forced the whole party off the Exchange, out at the north gate, opposite to Bartholomew-lane. They succeeded, however, after a desperate struggle in re-entering the Exchange; and having at length, with some further effort, effected a lodgment on one of the seats of the Exchange, they became once more visible, if not audible to the brokers, who surrounded them . . .'

Of the proliferating loans, schemes and 'bubbles', Professor R. A. Humphreys writes in his *Liberation in South America*: 'There were companies and plans to navigate the rivers of South America by steamboats, to fish for pearls in Colombia, to establish the "unemployed poor" of Great Britain and Ireland as agricultural colonists in the United Provinces of the Rio de la Plata . . . There was a company which proposed to export milkmaids to Buenos Aires in order to make butter, and a company was projected, its aims unspecified, to operate in Brazil, whose directors obligingly undertook to employ their capital in any profitable undertaking that might present itself.'

Among all these rash speculations, mines were the most alluring. The publication and wide circulation of Baron von Humboldt's account of his travels in South America between 1799 and 1804 had given new life to ideas of an El Dorado and of gold and silver to be had for the taking, and the argument ran that the mines deserted by the Spaniards during the revolution or abandoned because of primitive working methods might be rejuvenated by the introduction of modern steam-driven machinery and the employment of skilled Cornish or German miners. What the speculators, John Parish Robertson among them, failed to take into account was the extreme practical difficulty of transporting the machinery across the Andes or of settling Cornish miners in the wilds of Peru.

General Miller, as Prefect of Potosí, saw matters in more sober light:

'The society was further improved and enlivened by an influx of gentlemen, who came attended by a numerous civil staff, to bargain for mines, or to take possession of others purchased in London, sometimes of persons who had as much right to dispose of them as of so many square leagues of ocean.' Continuing in ironic vein, the *Memoirs* report on an English 'Grand Commissioner', described as 'the representative of a board of peers and princes, and to be amply furnished with the means, and duly empowered to buy up *all* the mines of Peru'; but their full sarcasm is reserved for a 'HEAD commissioner, who crossed the Pampas on the wings of the wind; scaled the Andes with *speed*, and gave to his descriptions the *vividness* of lightning; who rode a race of six thousand miles against time, and came in a-HEAD; [and] who on his return to England, gave to *his high-minded* employers, seated on velvet cushions around directorial boards, ROUGH NOTES instead of polished ingots . . .' The final conclusion is that 'in the end, empty pockets were found to be the natural consequence of empty heads'.

Despite his knowledge of South America, John Parish Robertson came to grief, like most of his competitors. The concessions of his Famatina Mining Company were disputed by a rival concern, and the miners sent out to work for it were first shipwrecked in the River Plate and then detained in Montevideo during the war between Brazil and the United Provinces; while the Pasco Peruvian Mining Company paid over the odds for its mines and had to sell the equipment to meet expenses. The Robertsons had meanwhile received £120,000 as their share in floating a £1,000,000 loan for the United Provinces of Buenos Aires – 'pretty pickings' as they were later described by a representative of Barings Bank, which had financed it – but both this and the Peruvian loans were to run into difficulties (the Peruvian government discontinued interest payments on its bonds in October 1825).

What proved to be the Robertsons' final undoing was a scheme for settling two hundred Scottish families on a tract of land south of Buenos Aires to be provided by the government. The first emigrants sailed from Leith in May 1825, and an official report issued three years later notes that 'This progressive and interesting society contains 326 inhabitants, including 85 children . . . The industry of the colonists is truly praiseworthy, and this little community preserve all the sober and moral habits of their own country. Butter and cheese are exclusively supplied to Buenos Aires . . .' A Mr Tweedie had 'invented an ingenious machine for clearing off the thistles; it is so effective that the national emblem can scarcely be any longer seen'; and the report concludes that 'The proprietors of the colony always found the members of it reasonable and contented, and feel every confidence in ultimate and entire success'. Nevertheless, the experiment was wound up in 1828, when the Robertsons, who had ultimately to buy the land at a cost of £60,000, ran out of funds.

Both their Lima and Buenos Aires houses were now forced into liquidation, and the Robertsons, who had made and lost a fortune in South America, left for England. It is said that John Parish had gone to Buenos Aires in the first place with only a guinea in his pocket and he returned to eke out his last days as a writer and journalist, dying at Calais in 1843.

The rise and fall of two other well-known Scottish traders, Maxwell and Wellwood Hyslop, followed somewhat similar lines – although complicated by the chequered fortunes of the patriots in Venezuela and New Granada. Underwritten by their cousins, W. and A. Maxwell & Co. of Liverpool, the brothers established a profitable business in Jamaica – where Maxwell befriended the penniless Bolívar in 1815 – exporting butter, soap, earthenware, hams and cheese, and shipping bacon, rum, logwood, coffee and cocoa, pimiento and indigo, ginger and cotton. A branch was established in Cartagena on the coast of New Granada, but its operations were abruptly terminated when General Morillo recaptured the city and Wellwood was thrown into prison, remaining there for four months until he was freed through the good offices of Admiral Douglas, commander of the Navy's Jamaica station.

The Hyslops rode out the storm, re-establishing their house in Cartagena, forming a branch at Maracaibo in 1821 and acting as agents for the government of Colombia in Jamaica. There was talk of their acting as contractors for a canal or railway to be built across the isthmus of Panama, but relations with their cousins in Liverpool had meanwhile cooled. Like the Robertsons, they finally came to grief over a government loan, when they were caught short after B. A. Goldschmidt & Co., the contractors for the Colombian government, suspended payments in January 1826.

If, in the last resort, the Robertsons and the Hyslops turned out to be spectacular losers in what the British Consul-General in Peru later described as 'a game of lottery', and imprudent investors in London lost their shirts by subscribing to mining shares or government loans (on which every government had discontinued payment of interest by the end of 1827), a host of less flamboyant traders had established a firm basis for a British commercial supremacy in South America, which was to last until the increasing penetration of the area by North American interests during the present century. By 1826 between eighty and a hundred British firms had established themselves in the former Spanish provinces. Peru had been flooded with British goods; most of Chile's needs were supplied by Britain and British India; while in Buenos Aires the 3000-strong British community reputedly owned most of the best property and had taken over half of the public debt.

In *The British in South America*, published in 1878, Michael Mulhall, who settled in Buenos Aires and made his living as a journalist, supplies some interesting side-lights on the flourishing British community during its early days. So, 'Blondel's guide of Buenos Aires for 1829 shows 49 English and American mercantile firms: the other English establishments comprised 18 grocer's shops, 4 hotels, 9 cabinet-makers, 3 upholsterers, 2 "barraqueros" [warehousemen], 2 livery stables, 3 blacksmiths, 1 broker, 1 auctioneer, 2 printing-offices, 4 house-painters, 1 jeweller, 5 huxters, 4 watchmakers, 5 apothecaries, 8 physicians, 6 tailors, 2 saddlers, 2 bootmakers, 3 hatters, 1 tinsmith and 1 brewer' – but it evidently took time for a taste for English beer to catch on, since the first brewery started by a Mr John Dillon about 1810 proved a failure.

The clerks in the British counting houses were all English or Scottish, 'except one native clerk in each house', but were 'poorly paid'. English mechanics, on the other hand, 'earned good wages, nearly 1*l* sterling per day'. One of the first doctors, Dr Oughan, had been Surgeon in Chief to the Peruvian army; while the spiritual needs of the Anglican community were looked after by the Rev. John Armstrong, who arrived in 1825. The large Scots community was ministered to by the Rev. William Brown, who founded a chapel and school at the Robertson brothers' model farm in 1827, finally retiring 'after 24 years of zealous pastorship' to his native St. Andrews, where he was Professor of Divinity until his death in 1868.

A regular packet line was begun in April 1824 with the clipper *Countess of Chichester*, 'which made a fair run out from England, and was beaten by the *Lord Hobart*, which took only 47 days; fare 80*l*'; and 'the month of August 1826 was memorable for two events; the foundation of the *British Packet*' – which under the editorship of a Mr Love was to relay news to the British residents for twenty-seven years – 'and for the institution of a British Amateur Theatrical society, for the relief of widows and orphans . . .'

Love was also the manager of the Buenos Aires Commercial Rooms, a favourite rendezvous of the British merchants, 'being supplied with English newspapers and reviews, maps, charts, telescopes, etc.: the members (56 in number) dining together at Faunch's hotel every quarter. Attached to the rooms was a library of 600 English volumes'. From 1824 until 1835 Faunch's held public banquets on St. Andrew's Day and also catered for the English on St. George's Day; while the Americans celebrated at the rival establishment of a Mrs Thorn on 4 July. Larger receptions were held at Wilde's Garden, some four acres in extent and 'tastefully laid out with teahouse, ball-rooms, fireworks etc. There was also a circus with 1200 seats. The whole was under the direction of Mr Bernard, and masqued balls were held at intervals. On the accession of Louis Philippe the French residents had a banquet here, the gardens being lit with Chinese lanterns' – but, sadly, 'The venerable Dean Funes, the historian, used to frequent the gardens, and was one day found dead, seated on his usual bench'.

Buenos Aires, as one of the main gateways to South America, clearly benefited from the coming of the foreign merchants. The wider question remains: to what extent did their intervention further the cause of liberation and subsequent development of the new and independent countries?

Agricultural areas, such as Chile and the great stock-raising hinterland of the Rio de la Plata enjoyed an enormous new demand for their products and a consequent inflow of foreign goods and currency. On the other hand, between 1819 and 1825, the silver-producing region of Peru shipped bullion to London alone to the value of some $27,000,000 in exchange for arms and consumer goods; and British consular reports of the period put the commercial capital of the country in 1826 at only a fifteenth of its amount in 1800. And here, as elsewhere, imports such as wine and cotton goods had a depressing effect on local producers.

In compiling his brother's *Memoirs*, John Miller came to the somewhat harsh opinion that the European merchants 'often assumed rather more credit than they were entitled to, from the circumstances of their happening to be the consignees of a few old ships, and of second-hand shops and stores. As men of business, indeed, these gentlemen were right to make the most of the market and their commodities; but then their claims to ardent patriotism, unmixed with views of profit, must be disallowed. It is true that many of them displayed the liberality of feeling which is generally found to exist in the commercial world; but in this case their sympathies and interest went hand in hand. When these became unhappily at variance, poor Sympathy often went to the wall . . .'

On the subject of the famous loans he is no less downright, being of opinion that they 'have turned out to be more prejudicial than useful to Chile and Peru, and will . . . continue to press like an incubus on those countries in their future efforts, to surmount the difficulties which the loans have themselves created . . .'

As a glaring example of the misuse of a loan, he points out that Chile, alone and unaided, succeeded in amassing a powerful fleet for the liberation of Peru, either by seizure of Spanish shipping or by the purchase of foreign vessels funded by 'bills, taken by the custom-house in payment of duties, and therefore nearly as good to the merchants as ready money'. A few years later the victorious squadron was rotting in port; and 'O'Higgins has been heard to say, that when he could only manage to raise supplies to meet the exigencies of the day, he was permitted to remain undisturbed for six years at the head of affairs; in which period Chile became not only one of the family of nations, but sent forth an expedition which laid the foundations of the independence of Peru. But the expectation of the arrival of the first instalment in gold from London caused rival candidates to spring up, and O'Higgins was induced to give way to men, under whose successive administrations the power and respectability of the republic have been almost uniformly retrograding.'

In monetary terms the nominal value of the British loans to the different South American states was in all more than £21,000,000; but the loans were not fully subscribed, and the amount which actually reached the governments has been estimated at about £12,000,000. The United Provinces of Buenos Aires, for example, incurred a debt of £1,000,000 in return for £600,000 in cash, most of it spent not on productive purposes, but in pursuing the war with Brazil. All in all, it is difficult to escape the conclusion that without the loans and the arms and other stores earlier supplied by the foreign merchants, the war would have been considerably prolonged; and the subsequent loss of confidence in South American investments cannot wholly be placed at the door of the governments concerned. It was also in large part caused by the greed of merchants and investors, who, in the words of a British consul-general in Peru, had chosen to 'embark in speculations at a period of eminent risk'.

Perhaps the last word can be left to Miller's *Memoirs*: '. . . speaking of the merchants as a body, and within the sphere of their counting houses, their pretensions to disinterested liberalism fall to the ground. But speaking of them individually, a very great many may be instanced as having given unequivocal proofs of their zeal and adherence to the cause of independence. When the destiny of Chile depended upon the uncertain chances of a battle, some English merchants [among them John Bagg, Samuel Haigh, Richard Price, James Barnard and William Hodgson] armed themselves, joined the patriot cavalry as volunteers, and participated in the brilliant charge which, at Maypo, decided the fate of the country. To such feats of gallantry might be added some splendid acts of philanthropy and benevolence, which reflect particular honour on the parties concerned. It was such conduct, and not assistance bestowed in the way of business, which caused the British to be looked up to with distinguished consideration.'

Epilogue
'BY GOD They shALL BE hAPPY!'

LOOKING at South America today, with its extremes of wealth and poverty, its vast but unevenly exploited resources and its propensity for short-lived military dictatorships, it seems relevant to ask what in fact the War of Independence actually achieved.

All the Liberators, to borrow Richard Ford's phrase, wore 'the blood-coloured cap of the much prostituted name of liberty' — but in what did liberty consist? To be more specific, the aims of the revolution at one time or another embraced: national and economic independence, religious tolerance, the abolition of forced labour, some form of unity within the area and the absence of foreign intervention, and the right of individuals to form governments of their own choosing.

In only one respect, the severing of political ties with Spain and Portugal, were these aims fully achieved. The fate of three prime movers of the revolution tells its own story: Bolívar died a disappointed man after his plans for a Gran Colombia and an association of the states in a loose Pan-American union had alike collapsed; O'Higgins was forced into exile in Peru, when vested interests rejected his schemes for a fairer division of land, popular education and the formation of a reserve for the Indians; while San Martín, so given to self-doubt and procrastination during his later days and averse to imposing a form of government on a society that was deeply divided, retired from Peru without completing its liberation.

O'Higgins put the central dilemma in a nut-shell when, coming to the conclusion that the uneducated were incapable of exercising a meaningful vote, yet determined that if they could not see what was good for them it must be forced upon them, he exclaimed 'By God they *shall* be happy!' In fact, in the full flush of revolution, the South Americans faced a problem insoluble at the time. Starting out with a resolve to cut loose from the corrupt civilization of Europe, they were too deeply imbued with the authoritarianism of Old Spain to find an acceptable alternative. Democracy, for what it was worth, had proved workable in Britain and North America because there was a climate of individual liberty and standards of education entirely lacking among the great mass of people in the new states.

Hence Bolívar was driven to the reluctant conclusion that, in the first place, some form of benevolent dictatorship was necessary to avoid a state of anarchy. His successor in Venezuela, General Páez, later observed that three kinds of actor appeared on the scene at independence: ex-soldiers who tended to severity and tyranny; those who had taken no part in the fighting but wanted to rule and slandered their former companions; and members of an 'Establishment', determined to maintain their traditional privileges. In effect, power now passed from a Spanish to a predominantly creole hierarchy, which, if native-born and bred, still ruled in the interests of a small minority of the well-to-do.

In 1890 an English visitor to the Argentine, Theodore Child, could still write that 'Owing to the lamentable want of public morality south of the equator and to the cynicism of the political vultures who make it their business to prey upon their fatherland, it is always a painful task to speak about the administration of the South American Republics' and also commented on the sad plight of hundreds and thousands of 'simple-minded workers'. Although certain countries, such as Venezuela and Cuba, are now tackling these problems in their very different ways, his critique, for all its somewhat lordly late-Victorian overtones, remains true of many South American countries a hundred and fifty years after the end of the wars of liberation.

The immediate and most tangible result of the indirect British participation was the capture by British merchants of the lion's share of the new South American markets. During the first three-quarters of the nineteenth century most of the finance for new development came from London, and British engineers and construction companies pioneered railways, canals, docks, foundries, gas works, water supplies and telephones. The United States began to take a more active part in investing in the area during the last decades of the century – though American engineers, like the famous Henry Meiggs, a fugitive from Californian justice, who built the first railways in Chile and Peru, had moved in rather earlier. With the advent of the two World Wars the British lost ground to the U.S.A., which has never been regained.

On the wider implications of British involvement in the struggle for independence, the Pan American Centennial Congress passed the following resolution as late as 1926:

'The Congress of Bolívar, Commemorative Congress of 1826, *considering*:

'That Great Britain lent to the liberty of Spanish America not only the support of its diplomacy, represented by Canning, but also an appreciable contingent of blood, and it may be asserted that there was no battlefield in the War of Independence on which British blood was not shed.

'That the heroic collaboration is made more brilliant by the decisive bravery of the British Legion in the battle of Carabobo; by the admirable loyalty of the British Aides of Bolívar, whose model was Ferguson, killed in the defence of the Liberator, at the post of duty; by the actions of MacGregor, Rooke, Brown, Guise and a hundred more; by the intrepid bravery of Cochrane and the battling constancy of William Miller of Peru.

'That later on the British Heroes who survived the epopee of liberty, incorporated themselves in the life of our democracies and also set through their austerity and love for order and institutions the highest civic examples.

'That finally it was such Britishers as O'Leary, Miller, O'Connor and Stevenson who laid the basis of the history of South America by collecting for posterity the first fragments of the immense Bolivian legend.

'*It is resolved*:

'That the Bolivian Congress, commemorative of the Congress of 1826, gratefully pays tribute and homage to the memory of the British Heroes who gave their lives or fought without compensation except their love of Liberty and Glory, in favor of the Independence of Spanish America.'

After a century's interval it was the most generous of compliments.

	EUROPE	UNITED PROVINCES & BANDA ORIENTAL	CHILE
1806		Seizure and loss of Buenos Aires by Sir Home Popham.	
1807	Junot enters Lisbon; The Portuguese royal family sails for Brazil; Napoleon orders the military occupation of Spain.		
1808	Napoleon obtains Ferdinand VII's abdication at Bayonne; Joseph Bonaparte becomes King of Spain; Britain enters the Peninsular War.		
1810	Summoning of the Cadiz Cortes.	Formation of Liberal Junta in Buenos Aires.	Deposition of the Spanish viceroy and formation of a Liberal Junta.
1811		Francia declares independence of Paraguay.	
1812	Promulgation of the liberal Spanish constitution. Castlereagh becomes British Foreign Secretary.		Coup of the Carrera brothers.
1813	Wellington defeats Joseph Bonaparte at Vitoria; the French evacuate Spain.		O'Higgins assumes power.

COMPARATIVE CHRONOLOGY

	PERU & BOLIVIA	VENEZUELA & NEW GRANADA	BRAZIL
1807			Arrival of Dom John and the Portuguese court in Rio de Janeiro.
1808			Opening of Brazilian ports for trade with friendly nations.
1810		Formation of Liberal Junta in Caracas; Bolívar returns from London to Venezuela.	Treaty of Commerce and Navigation with Great Britain.
1811	Patriot defeats in Upper Peru.		
1812		Betrayal and death of Francisco Miranda; flight of Bolívar to Curaçao.	
1813		Bolívar issues his decree of 'War to the death'; capture of Caracas. Bolivar named Liberator and Dictator.	

THE NEW CONQUISTADORS

	EUROPE	UNITED PROVINCES & BANDA ORIENTAL	CHILE
1814	Napoleon abdicates and Ferdinand VII returns to Spain.	Brown attacks the Spanish in the Plate; fall of Montevideo to Alvear; San Martín begins recruiting his Army of the Andes.	The patriots are defeated at Rancagua; the Spanish reoccupy Santiago.
1815	Battle of Waterloo.	Artigas captures Montevideo; Brown's expedition to the Pacific.	
1816		Congress of Tucumán; the United Provinces declare themselves independent.	
1817		Capture of Montevideo by the Portuguese.	Defeat of the Spanish by the Army of the Andes at Chacabuco; O'Higgins becomes Supreme Director.
1818			Defeat of the Spaniards at Maipú frees most of the country; arrival of Cochrane and his first cruise along the shores of Chile and Peru.
1819	British Foreign Enlistment Act.		

	PERU & BOLIVIA	VENEZUELA & NEW GRANADA	BRAZIL
1814	San Martín takes over command from Belgrano.	Spanish gains and loss of Caracas; Bolívar seeks refuge in Curaçao and Jamaica.	
1815	Patriot defeat at Sipe-Sipe.	Arrival of Morillo and Spanish counter-offensive.	Brazil granted dominion status within the Portuguese empire.
1816		Bolívar's unsuccessful expedition to Venezuela.	Portuguese attack on the Banda Oriental.
1817		Bolívar begins his final and successful campaigns in Venezuela and New Granada. Arrival of first British troops.	
1819		Battle of Boyacá. Bolívar proclaims Republic of Gran Colombia. Arrival of British and Irish Legions.	

	EUROPE	UNITED PROVINCES & BANDA ORIENTAL	CHILE
1820	Riego's *pronunciamento* and mutiny of the Spanish army at Cadiz; Ferdinand VII accepts Constitution of 1812.		Cochrane captures Valdivia; the expedition to free Peru sails from Valparaiso under San Martín and Cochrane.
1822	Death of Castlereagh; Canning becomes British Foreign Secretary.		Cochrane and San Martín return to Chile after liberating Lima.
1823	Ferdinand VII regains full power and annuls the reforms of 1820–3; the Polignac Memorandum; Monroe Doctrine promulgated in the U.S.A.		The Valparaiso earthquake; Cochrane sails for Brazil; O'Higgins resigns and retires to Peru.

	PERU & BOLIVIA	VENEZUELA & NEW GRANADA	BRAZIL
1820	San Martín's expedition lands in Peru. The cutting out of the *Esmeralda* by Cochrane.		
1821	The patriots occupy Lima. San Martín proclaimed Protector.	Battle of Carabobo secures Venezuelan independence. Bolívar elected President of Gran Colombia.	Departure of Dom John for Portugal; Dom Pedro becomes Regent of Brazil; the Lisbon Côrtes attempt to limit his authority.
1822	San Martín's meeting with Bolívar at Guayaquil. He abdicates and returns to Chile and from thence goes into exile in Europe.	The Battles of Bomboná and Pichincha secure the independence of Ecuador.	Dom Pedro declares Brazilian independence.
1823	Campaigns of Miller and Sucre in the Puertos Intermedios. Arrival of Bolívar in Peru.	The last Spanish troops in Venezuela surrender.	Arrival of Cochrane in Rio de Janeiro; he captures Bahia and pursues the Portuguese fleet across the Atlantic. Capture of Maranham and Pará by Cochrane's squadron. Dissolution of the Brazilian Assembly by Dom Pedro.
1824	Defeat of the Spaniards at Junín and Ayacucho.		Cochrane sails north to quell rebellions in the northern provinces.

THE NEW CONQUISTADORS

	EUROPE	UNITED PROVINCES & BANDA ORIENTAL	CHILE
1825	Portugal recognizes the independence of Brazil.	Juan Lavelleja crosses into the Banda Oriental with 'the immortal thirty-three'. Brazil declares war on the United Provinces.	
1826		Brown resumes command of the Buenos Airean squadron.	
1827		Brown defeats a Brazilian fleet at Juncal, but is later beaten at Monte Santiago.	

	PERU & BOLIVIA	VENEZUELA & NEW GRANADA	BRAZIL
1825	Surrender of last Spanish troops in Upper Peru; it is renamed Bolivia under the presidency of Sucre.	The Congress of Panama.	Cochrane returns to England; Brazil declares war on the United Provinces.
1826	The fall of Callao to the patriots.		
1828			Brazil and the United Provinces suspend hostilities and agree the independence of Uruguay at the instigation of Lord Ponsonby.
1830		Resignation and death of Bolívar.	

Further Reading

For additional background material the reader is referred to the bibliographies of such books as *The Liberators* by Irene Nicholson and *A History of Latin America* by Hubert Herring, listed below.

An Officer late in the Colombian Service, *The Present State of Colombia*, London, 1827.

An Officer of the Colombian Navy, *Recollections of a Service of Three Years during the War of Extermination*, London, 1828.

Antepara, José María, *South American emancipation, documents historical and explanatory*, London, 1810.

Archivo de don Bernardo O'Higgins, Vols. 1–XXIX, Imprentaria Universitaria, Santiago, 1945–70.

Archivo de general Miranda, 24 vols., Caracas and La Habana, 1929–50.

Arguedas, Alcides, *Historia general de Bolivia*, La Paz, 1922.

Armitage, John, *The History of Brazil*, 2 vols., London, 1836.

Atlay, J. B., *The Trial of Lord Cochrane before Lord Ellenborough*, London, 1897.

Barcia Trelles, Augusto, *San Martín en América*, 3 vols., Buenos Aires, 1943–6.

Belaúnde, V. A., *Bolívar and the Political Thought of the Spanish American Revolution*, Baltimore, 1938.

Beverina, Juan, *La guerra contra el Imperio de Brasil*, 2 vols., Buenos Aires, 1927–8.

Las invasiones inglesas al Río de la Plata. Buenos Aires, 1939.

Bleiberg, Germán, ed., *Diccionario de historia de España*, 2nd. ed., Madrid, 1968.

Bosch, Felipe, *Historia naval Argentina*, Buenos Aires, 1962.

Brown, Capt. C., *Narrative of the Expedition to South America which sailed from England in 1817, for the service of the Spanish patriots*, London, 1819.

Brown, Guillermo, *Documentos del Almirante Brown*, publn. de la Comisión nacional de Homenaje al Almirante Guillermo Brown en el centenario de su muerte 1857–1957, 2 vols., Academia Nacional de la Historia Argentina, Buenos Aires, 1958–9.

Bunster, Enrique, *Lord Cochrane*, 3rd. ed., Santiago de Chile, 1966.

Campaigns and Cruises in Venezuela and New Granada, and in the Pacific Ocean, 1817–1830, 3 vols., London, 1831.

Cecil, Henry, *A Matter of Speculation: The Case of Lord Cochrane*, London, 1965.

Chesterton, George Laval, *A Narrative of Proceedings in Venezuela in South America in the Years 1819 and 1820*, London, 1820.

Clissold, Stephen, *Bernardo O'Higgins and the Independence of Chile*, London, 1968.

Cochrane, Capt. Charles Stuart, *Journal of a Residence and Travels in Colombia during the Years 1823 and 1824*, London 1825.

Dundonald, Thomas Cochrane, Tenth Earl of, *Autobiography of a Seaman*, London, 1860.

Narrative of Services in the Liberation of Chili, Peru and Brazil, London, 1859.

Fortescue, J. W., *Dundonald*, London, 1906.

García, Rodolfo, 'Maria Graham no Brasil', in *Anais da Biblioteca Nacional do Rio de Janeiro*, Vol. LX, 1938.

Gillespie, Major Alexander, *Gleanings and Remarks Collected during Many Months of Residence at Buenos Ayres*, Leeds, 1818.

Gotch, Rosamund Brunel, *Maria, Lady Callcott*, London, 1937.

Graham, Gerald S. and Humphreys, R. A., eds., *The Navy and South America*, Navy Records Society, London, 1962.

Graham, Maria (Lady Callcott), *Journal of a Residence in Chile*, London, 1824.

Journal of a Voyage to Brazil, London, 1824.

Griffin, C. C., *The United States and the Disruption of the Spanish Empire, 1810–1822*, New York, 1937.

Hackett, James, *Narrative of the Expedition which sailed from England in 1817 to join the South American patriots*, London, 1818.

Haigh, Samuel, *Sketches of Buenos Ayres, Chile and Peru*, London, 1831.

Hall, Capt. Basil, *Extracts from a Journal written on the Coasts of Chili, Peru, and Mexico*, 2 vols., London, 1824.

Hasbrouck, Alfred, *Foreign Legionaries in the Liberation of Spanish America*, New York, 1928.

Herring, Hubert, *A History of Latin America*, 3rd. ed., London, 1968.

Hidy, R. W., *The House of Baring in American Trade and Finance*, Cambridge, Mass., 1949.

Hippisley, G., *Narrative of the Expedition to the Rivers Orinoco and Apuré*, London, 1819.

Holstein, Gen. H. L. V. Ducoudray, *Memoirs of Simon Bolívar*, London, 1830.

Humbolt, Alexander von, *Personal Narrative of Travels to the Equinoctial Regions of the New Continent During the Years 1799–1804*, tr. H. M. Williams, 7 vols., London, 1814–29.

Humphreys, R. A., ed., *British Consular Reports on the Trade and Policies of Latin America, 1824–1826*, London, 1940.

'British Merchants and South American Independence', in *Proceedings of the British Academy*, Vol. 51, 1965.

Liberation in South America: The Career of James Paroissien, London, 1952.

Iturbide, Agustin de, *Agustin de Iturbide*, London, 1824.

Kaufmann, William W., *British Policy and the Independence of Latin America, 1804–1828*, New Haven, 1951.

Lecuna, Vicente, *Cartas del Libertador*, 10 vols., Venezuelan Government, Caracas, 1939.

Documentos referentes a la creación de Bolivia, 2 vols., Caracas, 1925.

La entravista de Guayaquil, Caracas, 1948.

Lloyd, Christopher, *Lord Cochrane*, London, 1947.

Madariaga, Salvador de, *Bolívar*, London, 1952.

Maia, Prado, *A Marinha de Guerra do Brasil na Colonia e no Império*, Rio de Janeiro, 1965.

Manchester, Alan K., *British Preeminence in Brazil, Its Rise and Decline*, Chapel Hill, North Carolina, 1933.

Mawe, John, *Travels in the Interior of Brazil*, London, 1812.

M'Gregor, Sir Gregor, *An Account of the Late Expedition against the Isthmus of Darien*, London, 1821.

Miers, John, *Travels in Chile and La Plata*, 2 vols., London, 1826.

Miller, John, *Memoirs of General Miller in the Service of the Republic of Peru*, 2 vols., London, 1828.

Mitre, Bartolomé, *Historia de Belgrano y de la independencia argentina*, 3 vols., 3rd. ed., Buenos Aires, 1876–7.

Historia de San Martin y de la emancipación sud-americana, 4 vols., 2nd. ed., Buenos Aires, 1890.

Mulhall, Michael G., *The English in South America*, Buenos Aires, N. D. (1878).

Narrative of a voyage to the Spanish Main in the Ship 'Two Friends', London, 1819.

Nicholson, Irene, *The Liberators*, London, 1969.

O'Connor, Fráncisco Burdett, *Independencia americana*, Madrid, Biblioteca Ayacucho, N.D.

O'Leary, Daniel Florence, *Memorias*, 6 vols., Caracas, Imprenta Nacional, 1952.

Opazo Maturana, Gustavo, 'Lady Cochrane en Chile', in *Boletín de la Academia Chilena de la Historia*, X, No. 25, 1943.

Otero, J. P., *Historia del libertador Don José de San Martín*, 4 vols., Buenos Aires, 1932.

Páez, José Antonio, *Autobiografía del General José Antonio Páez*, 2 vols., New York, 1878.

Paz Soldán, Mariano Felipe, *Historia de Perú independiente*, 3 vols., Lima, 1868.

Pendle, George, 'British Adventurers in the South American Wars of Independence', in *History Today*, Vol. X, No. 4, 1960.

Pereira da Silva, J. M., *Historia da Fundacão do Imperio Brazileiro*, 7 vols., Rio de Janeiro, 1864.

Pilling, William, *The Emancipation of South America*, London, 1893. (This is a translation and abridgement of Mitre's *Historia de San Martin, op. cit.*).

Proctor, Robert, *Narrative of a Journey across the Cordillera of the Andes and of a Residence in Lima*, London, 1825.

Rafter, M., *Memoirs of Gregor M'Gregor*, London, 1820.

Ratto, Héctor, *Historia del Almirante Guillermo Brown*, Buenos Aires, 1939.

Vida de Brown, Buenos Aires, 1943.

Los Comodores britanicos de estación en el Plata, Buenos Aires, 1945.

Read, Jan, '"Independence or Death", British Adventurers in South America', in *History Today*, Vol. XXV, No. 6, 1975.

Lord Cochrane, Caracas (Plata Press Biographies), 1978.

Rippy, J. F., *British Investment in Latin America, 1822–1949*, Minneapolis, 1959.

Roberts, Carlos, *Las invasiones inglesas del Río de la Plata*, Buenos Aires, 1938.

Robertson, J. P. and Robertson, W. P., *Letters on Paraguay*, 3 vols., London, 1838–9.

Robertson, W. S., *France and Latin American Independence*, Baltimore, 1939.

Rodriguez Villa, Antonio, *El teniente general Don Pablo Morillo primer conde de Cartagena, Marqués de la Puerta*, 3 vols., Madrid, 1908–10.

Rubio, J. M., *La infanta Carlota Joaquina y la politica de España en America (1808–1812)*, Madrid, 1920.

Salcedo-Bastardo, J. L., *Bolívar, A Continent and its Destiny*, London, 1977.

Sherwell, Guillermo A., *Antonio José de Sucre*, Caracas, 1973.

Stevenson, William Bennet, *A Historical and Descriptive Narrative of Twenty Years' Residence in South America*, 3 vols., London, 1825.

Street, John, *Artigas and the Emancipation of Uruguay*, Cambridge, 1959.

Temple, Edmond, *Travels in Various Parts of Peru, including a year's residence in Potosi*, London, 1830.

The Proceedings of a General Court Martial for the Trial of Lieut. Gen. Whitelock, 2 vols., London, 1808.

The Retired Governor of Juan Fernandez, *Sixteen Years in Chile and Peru from 1822–1839*, London, N.D.

Tute, Warren, *Cochrane: A Life of Admiral the Earl of Dundonald*, London, 1965.

Vicuña Mackenna, B., *The First Britons in Valparaiso, 1817–27*, Valparaiso, 1884.

Weatherhead, W. Davidson, *An Account of the late expedition against the isthmus of Darien under the command of Sir Gregor M'Gregor*, London, 1821.

Webster, C. K., ed. *Britain and the Independence of Latin America 1812–1830, Selected Documents from the Foreign Office Archives*, 2 vols., London, 1938.

Whitaker, A. P., *The United States and the Independence of South America, 1800–1830*, Baltimore, 1941.

Index

171